Client-Centered Consulting

Client-Centered Consulting

Getting Your Expertise Used When You're Not in Charge

Peter Cockman, Bill Evans, and Peter Reynolds

McGraw-Hill

New York   San Francisco   Washington, D.C.   Auckland   Bogotá
Caracas   Lisbon   London   Madrid   Mexico City   Milan
Montreal   New Delhi   San Juan   Singapore
Sydney   Tokyo   Toronto

Library of Congress Cataloging-in-Publication Data
Cockman, Peter
    Client-centered consulting: a practical guide for internal
advisers and trainers / Peter Cockman, Bill Evans, and Peter
Reynolds.
        p.   cm.—(McGraw-Hill training series)
    Includes bibliographical references and index.
    1. Business consultants.   2. Education consultants.
3. Consultants.   I. Evans, Bill.   II. Reynolds, Peter.   III. Title.
IV. Series.
HD69.C6C56   1992   92-11970
001'.068'3—dc20   CIP

McGraw-Hill

*A Division of The **McGraw·Hill** Companies*

First published © 1992, McGraw-Hill International (UK) Limited

    4 5 6 7 8 9 10   FGRFGR   9 9 8

ISBN 0-07-707565-X

This book is printed on recycled, acid-free paper containing a
minimum of 50% recycled, de-inked fiber.

McGraw-Hill books are available at special quantity discounts to use as
premiums and sales promotions, or for use in corporate training programs. For more information, please write to the Director of Special
Sales, McGraw-Hill, 11 West 19th Street, New York, NY 10011. Or contact
your local bookstore.

Contents

About the authors

The authors came together as internal consultants for British Gas in 1975. They developed and refined their ideas about the role and the training and development of internal advisers while working as consultants inside and outside the company. They continue to introduce their ideas into many organizations, working sometimes independently, sometimes together. This book is the culmination of many years' experience learning how to be client-centred themselves and helping others to work in a similar way.

Peter Cockman is a senior partner in the Stone Cockman Partnership, committed to helping companies to take up the total quality challenge and introduce more appropriate attitudes and management style. He has been actively involved in training and development for over 20 years as an internal and external consultant. His main interest and expertise is in helping managers to improve business results by recruiting and leading more effective teams and ensuring that members of their staff are involved and contribute to the best of their ability. To improve the service to managers he runs public and in-house workshops, helping internal advisers from industry and education to develop their skills as client-centred consultants.

Bill Evans founded Oxford Management Consultants in 1982, committed to the principles of client-centredness and the empowerment of people. These principles underpin all his work with internal consulting departments in organizations from manufacturing to education. He has considerable expertise in experiential approaches to training and finds some of his most rewarding work in helping other trainers to develop similar skills. He has been involved in a number of organizational change projects and has worked with several companies, helping them cope with the human aspects of Total Quality Management initiatives. He has written training packages for sales people and sales managers which are used throughout the world.

Peter Reynolds is an experienced personal counsellor working within organizations. He specializes in the management of stress at work, helping companies to set up initiatives to aid employees who have been the subject of robbery or violence in the workplace. He has published articles on counselling at work and currently divides his time between writing, his own consultancy work in the financial and service sectors and being a principal associate with Oxford Management Consultants.

He remains dedicated to extending the application of client-centred principles in all areas of consulting. He has a BA degree from the Open University and an MBA from Bradford University.

Preface

This book is addressed to all those thousands of people in various organizations and in a variety of professional disciplines across the country who find themselves having to help people, either individually or in groups, to be more effective without any authority over them or choosing not to use that authority.

Such people are required to advise, counsel, influence, persuade or sell ideas to the people they help—their clients—so that the problems they are working on get solved and stay solved. This requires them to think of themselves as *consultants*, to understand themselves and their clients, to have confidence in their own ability and a positive self-image.

We believe that being client-centred is the only way to operate, remembering that ultimately your clients always have a choice—to change or not to change. We believe that truly client-centred consultants work hard to empower their clients and support them right through to the point where the new behaviour replaces the old. But if, at the end of the day, your clients decide not to change then that is their prerogative.

In our experience, much of the work done by internal consultants focuses on a particular field of expertise, often to the exclusion of everything else. So the safety officer looks at unsafe practices, the systems analyst looks at the possibility of transferring work to the computer and the auditor looks at accounting procedures. These single-issue interventions seldom deal with the complete problem and often fail to have an impact on the total organization.

It is probably true that few internal consultants will be called in to deal with problems which focus on the development needs of the whole organization, but we believe it is possible for such consultants to extend their influence far beyond the narrow limits of the task they are often called upon to improve. They can extend the boundaries by always looking to see how the problem is being managed in terms of the systems and procedures, as well as looking at how people feel about the problem and everything surrounding it, and also collecting data about the technical/task aspects.

In the quest for continuing improvement the problem-solving process has become particularly important. Going through the stages—gathering data; analysing the data; generating solutions; selecting the solution; planning for implementation; implementing and then continuing to improve—has become an essential part of total quality management.

We believe that, for the first time, we have successfully integrated our ideas about the consulting process with the knowledge of how people learn and the problem-solving process.

We have tried to produce a 'how to do it' book on the assumption that most internal consultants learn consulting by trying it out in practice. We hope our readers will use this book as a guide rather than a book of instructions and then try out the ideas with their own clients.

We hope that our contribution will appeal to those who have been consultants for some time as well as those who are just starting. We have had great fun writing it and it has helped us to clarify our thoughts and integrate many of the ideas we have collected and developed over the years. We hope you will get as much from reading it as we have from writing it.

Peter Cockman   Bill Evans   Peter Reynolds

July 1991

Acknowledgements

We have based this book on our collective experience as internal consultants over many years in a variety of industrial companies and many years helping a range of internal consultants to be more effective. Since becoming independent external consultants we have all continued to develop and run consulting skills programmes for internal consultants from industry, commerce, central and local government, voluntary organizations and education.

When we first became internal consultants there was very little written to help us. Over the years we have been influenced by the work of Bob Blake and Jane Mouton in their book *Consultation*, by Gordon and Ronald Lippitt in *The Consulting Process in Action*, Gerard Egan in *The Skilled Helper* and *Face to Face*, by Ed Schien in *Process Consultation* and by Peter Block in *Flawless Consulting*. We owe a great deal to the inspiration of these eminent consultants.

We have also gained a great deal from the many hundreds of people who have taken part in the seminars and workshops we have run for internal consultants over the last 15 years. They have generously given of themselves to improve their knowledge and skill, thereby enabling us to do the same.

We are especially indebted to David Casey whose way of being with his clients (and us) showed us how to be truly client-centred.

We are also very grateful to all those colleagues who shared our value systems, our beliefs and our philosophy and worked with us to re-evaluate our approach to our clients and be much more client-centred with consultants in training. Many of them have progressed to be highly competent external consultants or to exercise considerable influence as senior consultants in their organizations. We hope that all the people we have listed will see this book as a way of saying 'Thank You' for the support they have given us:

Deidre D'Arcy	Trevor Arnoll	Mary Barry
Jim Borritt	Malcolm Bryce	Pam Chantry
David Clifford	David Collin	David Cranage
Malcolm Dawson	Gillian Dickinson	Kath Dowson
Roger Edwardson	Alan Forsdick	Dorothy Hale
Laura Hall	Peter Harvey	Gerry Hughes
Steve Hughes	Judy Hunter	Dave Jeffries
John Jellis	Gillian Jennings	Peter Joy

Sue Maggs	Jane Marsh	Andy Miller
Roger Moon	Rosemary Morris	Sue Mullally
Joy Packard	Mike Padgett	Sheila Phillips
Max Playfer	Robbie Robertson	John Rogers
Patricia Shaw	Kevyn Smith	Jane Sonntag
Pat Stewart	Beverley Stone	Brad Strachan
Gill Thomas	Tony Tyrrell	Rob Urwin
Sharon Usher	June Whitney	Alan Wilkins
Carol Williams	Len Young	Nick Zienau

We finally acknowledge the support and tolerance of our families while we wrote and rewrote the text. We also acknowledge the invaluable contribution of Alix Horne whose word processing skills have come to our rescue more than once. And last but not least our thanks to McGraw-Hill for offering us the opportunity to put our ideas into print.

1 Consultants, clients and the consulting process

What is consulting?

If you are reading this book you are likely to be an internal consultant, a change agent. You have been hired to facilitate change in your organization. It is your job to influence and advise people, to help them and persuade them to do things differently. You are likely to be asked to help people adapt to new technology, changes in the market-place or changes in the organizational structure. If you are successful, people's lives will be different when you have moved on. Making this sort of impact on an organization is difficult even if you are the chief executive with all the power incumbent in that position. But somebody has asked you to make your imprint on the organization and given you no formal authority over anyone. Indeed, you may well be in a comparatively lowly position. No one would blame you if you are feeling frustrated and powerless.

The purpose of this book is to let you explore ideas which will help you become more powerful in your organization by being client-centred.

First let us draw some comfort from the lessons of the past. The course of history is full of people who possessed tremendous political and military power—the Roman emperors, feudal kings, the Russian tsars and their successors. People like Napoleon, Hitler and Stalin have wielded immense power and certainly had a huge impact on the lives of people over whom they held sway. Their place in our collective memory is assured, yet their influence has been undermined and rejected by following generations.

History has also produced other people whose imprint on the world was profound and timeless, yet they all operated without any obvious power base. Jesus Christ and Mohammed touched the lives of millions across countless generations through their teaching and way of being. Socrates, Confucius and Plato still affect our lives because of what they wrote. In our time we would argue that Mikhail Gorbachev has had a much more profound effect on the world by renouncing the power of his office rather than enhancing his ability to control as his predecessors did. Others like Nelson Mandela, Mother Theresa, Martin Luther King and Mahatma Ghandi have all influenced the world without any power to control others.

In a different vein, another example of the power of the individual to influence millions can be seen in Bob Geldof. In a very brief time he galvanized the pop world and generated a ground swell of worldwide support which culminated in World Aid with massive repercussions for the Third World.

So from where do these great consultants, change agents of history, derive their power? First of all they have the ability to capture people's imagination so that others take ideas on board and make them their own. They are all people-centred with a mission to empower others rather than control them; they are sensitive to the needs of the people; they are not afraid on occasion to confront those in authority. In short, they are all client-centred.

The dictionary provides some fascinating meanings for the act of consultation. To consult is 'to ask advice of', 'to decide or act in favour of', 'to look up for information or advice', 'to consider jointly, to take counsel'. A consultation we are told is a 'meeting for conspiracy or intrigue'. Consulting is what you do to a physician or lawyer or anyone who is prepared to give professional advice to others in the same field.

For the purposes of this book we believe that consulting should be what happens when someone with a problem or difficulty seeks help to solve that problem or resolve that difficulty from someone who has special skill.

How is consulting different from counselling?

From our point of view a counsellor is someone who specializes in working with a single client or maybe a couple to help them with personal difficulties which they are experiencing in their lives. Counsellors may be part of an organization set up specifically to do this kind of work—Samaritans or Relate—or they may be people at work who happen to be good at listening to others. There are also many commercial organizations which have taken this problem seriously and appointed counsellors to work on such problems either full or part-time. Counselling—in the sense of helping people resolve problems in their personal life which affect or may affect their work—is often part of the job description of managers and supervisors. Where it is, they should receive special training to help them do it well.

For us counselling is a specialized form of consultancy which tends to be used with people who have personal problems which they find difficult or impossible to solve on their own. Consultants, especially client-centred consultants, sometimes find themselves in the role of counsellor during the course of their work in organizations. Indeed, we would argue that counselling skills should be part of the stock in trade of every effective client-centred consultant.

Who needs consulting skills?

By definition, a consultant is someone who takes part in a consultation and can be the person seeking help or the person providing it. Common usage, however, has the consultant as the person providing help. Although there is still some reluctance among the helping professions generally to accept the title of consultant, more and more people in advisory roles are beginning to perceive that this is what they are.

In addition to the classical consulting areas such as medicine and law the field has expanded enormously to include:

accounting and audit	personnel services
computing and information management	productivity services
corporate planning	quality control
industrial relations	research and development
occupational health	health and safety
operational research	training and development
organization development	vocational counselling

This means that anyone who is in a role where the main emphasis is on helping individuals, departments or organizations to be more effective in whatever they do can be fairly considered to be a consultant. Line managers are finding that they have more than enough to do keeping abreast of their current jobs and they need the help of a large number of specialists with the knowledge and skill to work with them to solve problems so that their department can be more effective in meeting its objectives. Also, as a result of increasing specialization in many walks of life, people in many specialist jobs find themselves being consultants for some of their time. For example:

communications	accounting
design	new systems
development	inspection
programming	marketing
public relations	sales

Furthermore, with the move towards collaboration and involvement at work and the need to gain commitment to change, managers themselves are beginning to act as consultants to their own staff whenever possible. When they interact with staff about their performance or development, talk to customers about their needs, or deal with the hundreds of consumer associations and community groups, they need the same skills as those who have more formal consultant roles.

So for our purposes consultants are:

People who find themselves having to influence other people, or advise them about possible courses of action to improve the effectiveness of any aspect of their operations, without any formal authority over them or choosing not to use what authority they have.

This can be described as a *consultant/client* relationship. It is present whether you find yourself helping managers to be more effective; helping teachers relate better to their pupils, to one another or to the headteacher; helping teams work better together; providing career guidance to pupils leaving school, graduates leaving university or women returning to work; or launching a major initiative to improve quality throughout an organization be it commercial, industrial or educational. Whether you are someone stopped in the corridor by a colleague saying 'Can I have a word with you?' or the Secretary General of the United Nations jetting across the world in an effort to avert global war—*you* are a consultant.

From our point of view, if you are involved for even part of your time in providing help to someone else, in whatever manner you do it you need consulting skills. We will offer you an opportunity to consider these skills and to assess the degree to which you have acquired them.

What is client-centred consulting?

Until comparatively recently the very term 'consultant' conjured up the idea of enormous expertise and experience based on impressive academic qualifications. Most people aspiring to be consultants had to demonstrate their unusual competence for solving problems and their personal and career success. This gave rise to the idea that consultants were people who diagnosed your problem and gave you a prescription to follow which in their opinion would solve your problem. Nowadays, effective consultants still have expertise and experience in solving problems; however, it is impossible to identify a consultant's qualifications by looking merely at academic success.

While many consultants seem to be in the business of dispensing small amounts of professional advice for very large fees (and in the process ensuring dependency) that is not our view of a healthy relationship with a client. That is not to say that there aren't times when the client wants and needs professional advice to solve a problem. If a piece of machinery breaks down what most people want is an expert to fix it so that it stays fixed. But, and we believe it is a big but, for each one of those there are hundreds of situations and problems which the client could solve with a little judicious help from a client-centred consultant who is not interested in fostering dependency but wants the client to be able to solve similar problems in future without recourse to the consultant.

This book is about consultants who are client-centred. They are presumed to have sufficient expertise in their own technical discipline, accounting, social science, health and safety, training and development, systems analysis, learning methods and teaching. What they have in addition is an extra competence in the process of consultation. They are also likely to have:

- a high level of self-awareness
- a thorough understanding of the ways in which clients are likely to behave as individuals and in groups
- a wide range of professional and interpersonal skills
- sufficient flexibility of style to deal with a variety of clients and situations
- a real understanding of the helping process within the context of their professional discipline

We believe that all consultants are more effective if they have a feeling of self-confidence which stems from adequate knowledge, skill and ability and consequently a positive self-image. We also believe that the majority of people called upon to be consultants are competent in the technical content of their own jobs and are usually familiar with the technical aspects of the jobs done by the people they are called upon to help. However, the effective use of that technical knowledge depends to a large extent upon the personal style of the consultant. The most effective consultants seem to be those who have worked on their personal styles to make them appropriate to the circumstances, particularly in the way they build relationships, identify problems and arrange implementation of solutions.

The ways of influencing and generally being sensitive and responsive to the needs and feelings of clients are at least as important and probably more important than technical expertise. It is our experience that when consultants and clients treat each other with mutual respect then the outcome is usually successful.

In summary, client-centred consulting is about:

- starting where the clients are, not where you think they are
- helping clients decide what data or information to collect
- allowing clients to diagnose their problem for themselves
- helping clients make sense of the data rather than doing it yourself
- providing theory to help clients make sense of the data or make decisions about courses of action
- helping clients gain commitment to the plan of action
- assisting clients to implement the decisions and arranging follow-up if appropriate
- disengaging responsibly as soon as possible
- ensuring that clients retain ownership of the problem and don't become dependent on you

How do I stay client-centred?

Consultation is an intervention designed to bring about change in an existing unsatisfactory set of circumstances to effect improvement. While many consultants take it upon themselves to decide what is right for the client and therefore get involved in influencing, persuading or directing the client into changed behaviour, the client-centred consultant does not operate this way. It is always possible for the client to terminate the consultation; the consultant, while having an opinion, leaves the client with the option to change or not. Thus the client-centred consultant is less likely to be manipulative in helping the client come to a decision about how to solve the problem. The client always has freedom of choice. This is not to say that the consultant shouldn't work very hard to ensure the client assesses the implications of not changing and considers the advantages and disadvantages of all the options for solving the problem. But the final decision about action or inaction should remain with the client. Particular circumstances in which the consultant might choose to impose a solution will be discussed in Chapter 2 on Intervention Styles.

Most behaviour, whether of an individual, members of a team or people in a larger organization or social system, follows standard patterns and is repetitive or cyclical in nature. In other words, behaviour repeats itself within specific situations and time-scales. Much of the time such standard patterns are useful: who would want people to experiment with driving on the opposite side of the road to everyone else just to see what it was like to change the cyclical nature of their behaviour pattern? But sometimes such behavioural patterns are not functional. What happens to the children who have been well schooled in how to cross the road in Britain when they go on a school trip to France? With any luck there will be feedback immediately they step off the kerb in the shape of screaming tyres and the gendarme's whistle. But this is not always the case with ineffective or cyclical behaviour in other circumstances, especially in organizations. Often ineffective behaviour patterns do not get challenged by the people working in the department or company. How many times have you heard the answer 'We've always done it that way' to the naive question 'Why do you do that?'.

The consultant's function is to challenge ineffective patterns of behaviour which are seen to be inhibiting effectiveness or change. When you come across operators continually making the same mistake, when you see a management group constantly ending meetings in uproar, when you witness the same breakdown in communication time after time, it is up to you, the consultant, to point out the incidence and implications of such cyclical behaviour and help the client replace it with more effective behaviour. The consultant's function is to help the client identify and break out of such damaging cycles of behaviour.

One way of looking at the levels of activity between client and consultant in the problem-solving process is illustrated by Lippitt and Lippitt

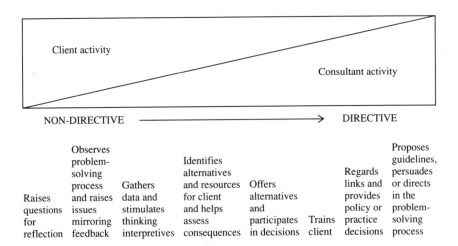

Figure 1.1 *Levels of client/consultant activity*
Adapted from Lippitt and Lippitt, *The Consulting Process in Action*, Pfeiffer & Company, San Diego, CA, 1978. Reproduced with permission of the publisher.

(1978) in Figure 1.1. All these styles of operating are valid and legitimate. The real difficulty facing the consultant is deciding how to use them appropriately.

At the directive end of the continuum shown in Figure 1.1 we find the consultant who has technical knowledge and expertise that the client lacks. It may be appropriate, therefore, to give the client advice or information to solve the immediate problem. This may be what you want when your car, television or computer has broken down. However, as Lippitt and Lippitt point out, 'research into the nature of the helping relationship suggests that dependency on the helper is not in the long-range interests of the client'. Having fixed the immediate problem it may be more appropriate to move towards the non-directive end and help the client learn how to avoid getting into similar difficulties in future, or how to rectify the malfunction without recourse to a consultant.

There seem to be two important dilemmas for the client-centred consultant. The first is 'How do I use my technical expertise and know-how without appearing to tell the client what to do?'. The second is 'How do I avoid being the "expert" who tells the client what to do, when the role is such a seductive one?'.

To address the first dilemma, the consultant should never withhold expertise and know-how from the client if, by withholding it, the problem doesn't get solved. However, we believe that the consultant is well advised to help the client see the consultant as a source of information which the client can use. If the client cannot see this then the consultant may have to 'bite the bullet' and be prescriptive. This is especially so if the client is in a desperate situation and has no idea what to do to solve the problem. But there are implications and you will have to decide whether the advantages outweigh the disadvantages in the particular situation at the time. However, giving advice early in the relationship may set up dependency and give rise to poor problem solving. Giving advice when the relationship has developed may be acceptable.

The second dilemma concerns how you feel about yourself and your client. If your personal power comes from being seen as an expert then you are likely to be very attracted to giving advice. Likewise, if you view your client as incompetent and helpless then you are likely to give advice. From the other side of the relationship the client may wish to be in the safe hands of an expert and therefore could ask for advice. Some of the following questions attempt to spring the trap on the pseudo client-centred consultant:

- What would you do in my position?
- You must have experience of such problems; what did you do?
- How do other people solve similar problems?
- I have no experience. I can't possibly solve this problem, can I?
- I'm new to this, can you just give me a few ideas?

This 'expert' trap is there whether you are giving advice on a technical task or the way a department is organized and managed. More will be said about these dilemmas in Chapter 2.

The training role can offer opportunities for powerful client-centred work. However, it is possible to train and educate entirely prescriptively. If the consultant diagnoses the difficulty, decides on the solution and trains the client accordingly, this doesn't seem to be very different from advice giving. But in the training and educating role the client-centred consultant helps the client to diagnose the difficulty, may offer theories, models or frameworks to help the client understand the difficulty and what to do about it and may then help the client implement the new methods or ways of working. However, the client always retains the ability to reject the particular theory or model or to adapt it to the particular situation. It follows, therefore, that client-centred consultants have to accept that their pet theories on how things should be done may end up in the bin. Commitment and belief in theories and models is very important—ownership is not!

Moving further towards the non-directive end of the Lippitts' continuum, we can start to identify a problem-solving approach that gives the client more involvement. This requires the consultant to work hard to stay out of the content of the problem, and help the client get some clarity about the problem and the options available. Such a role is entirely about being and staying client-centred. You are there to enable the client to see how many different problems make up the presenting problem, how many strands there are to the same problem and maybe how the presenting problem relates to the real problem. Once that has been done you can help the client to think about alternative courses of action to solve the problem, evaluate these alternatives and the implications and decide which one to choose. The client may need help to decide on a plan of action but the final plan should belong to the client rather than the consultant. It is important to note that this role is not about accepting all that the client says without question. There may be inconsistencies between what the client says and what the client does and this may need confronting. Overall, however, the consultant is there to help the client:

- perceive the situation more clearly
- devise alternative strategies for solving the problem
- evaluate the alternatives
- decide on a course of action (including doing nothing)
- plan the implementation and take action

At the extreme of the non-directive end the consultant stays entirely within the client's frame of reference and helps the client get a clearer understanding of the problem. This includes identifying any feelings which may be forming a block to logical problem solving. The client is therefore ultimately responsible for doing something about the problem or not. This is also the extreme of client-centred consulting. The consultant doesn't get involved in the problem, accepts the client as he or she is, works hard to establish a trusting and open relationship but does not give advice. Unless, of course, the client is absolutely floundering, when a prescriptive solution may be all that is left. What the consultant can and must do is to reflect back key words, summarize and paraphrase the client's thoughts and feelings.

While it will be obvious that a consultant can fulfil many roles during any one intervention (and may change from moment to moment) it is important to maintain client-centredness throughout if you wish to enhance your client's problem-solving ability and do not wish to be seen as an expert. In order to stay client-centred you need to address the following types of questions:

• Do I get defensive when challenged or confronted?
• Does my self-esteem depend upon being seen as an expert?
• Do I like giving advice to people to influence their behaviour?

That was just to get you in tune. A more complete checklist for client-centredness is given at the end of this chapter—you might like to try it now.

Who are clients?

If we go back to our dictionary we find that a client is described as 'a vassal, dependant or hanger-on, one who employs a lawyer or professional adviser, a customer'. This seems to suggest that anyone who has a problem or difficulty is a potential client. When people seek help to deal with some difficulty or to solve a problem by approaching someone they believe can provide help, they become clients. Hence it is possible to think of clients as people who approach doctors or lawyers for advice, those who seek technical expertise from a mechanic, or help from a psychotherapist or counsellor, or shoppers in a store seeking to satisfy their need for household goods or clothes.

Clients are often individuals seeking assistance for themselves. However, the client can also be a group, a department or an organization. As most consultants deal with more than one client, we find it more useful to think of a 'client system'. Even counsellors who work with an individual client often find that their client is part of a family or is in a relationship where his or her behaviour has an impact on someone else. Also, in organizations it is seldom the case that an individual can bring about any necessary change alone.

It is important not to define your client system too narrowly. You need to ask yourself which people are likely to be significantly affected by the changes. The answer may lead you to identify individuals or groups from other sections, other departments, or even other companies in different geographical locations. All these people are potentially part of your client system.

In summary then a client is:

• any individual, or group of people who need some kind of help from outside (the consultant) to work on a problem

- probably someone with whom the relationship is temporary—although some assignments can last for months or even years
- someone who enters into the relationship with the consultant on a voluntary basis

Do I have the real client?

Even when you have identified that there is more than one client or that there is a whole client system it is often quite difficult to know that you have reached the point where you are dealing with the real or total client system. Professor Reg Revans of 'action learning' fame (1980) has some very useful things to say about finding the real client. He talks about the artfulness of effective negotiation to find 'Who knows? Who cares? Who can?'. If we apply these three questions to finding out who our real client or client system is, we can ensure that we involve all three if they happen to be different.

Who knows—about the problem or has most of the information that we need to be able to diagnose and help solve the problem is often the person doing the job. The people working for the manager with the problem will often know most about what is going on. Unless we accept that they are part of the system we shall not get very far.

Who cares—that something is done about the problem might well be the manager with the problem. It is likely to be the manager who identified the problem or who is bearing the pain due to the ineffectiveness of the department. However, there may be other people who care about the problem who also have to be considered as part of the system.

Who can—do something about the solution? If those with the problem have to ask for authority or approval to implement the solution, if they need more resources in terms of money or time or people and someone else controls those resources, then you had better involve that person as part of the client system at the beginning. Otherwise, just as you are about to talk about implementation, someone may say they have to get board approval and by then it may be too late!

The client system is not complete until it includes everyone who is involved in the answers to the three vital questions: Who knows? Who cares? Who can?

An example we encountered might make the whole thing clear. An internal training adviser was called in by her personnel and training manager and given an assignment to provide training for a group of employees in another part of the organization. At this stage the work group had no knowledge of these intentions. To complicate matters the original request for training had come from the group's departmental manager who asked the personnel and training manager for help. Furthermore, the budget for such training was also controlled by the departmental manager. In this case, who is the client? Is it the personnel and training manager who made the initial request? Is it the departmental manager who wanted the training and controlled the budget? Or is it the group who were to be trained even if they didn't know it? Using Revans's ideas to find the real client or client system, the answers to the questions are as follows:

- *Who knows?*　Who knows there is a problem?—the departmental manager and the personnel and training manager
  Who knows the detail about the problem?—the departmental manager
  Who knows about sources of help?—the personnel and training manager
- *Who cares?*　Who cares enough to do anything about the problem?—the departmental manager and perhaps the personnel and training manager
- *Who can?*　Who can do anything about the problem?—the work group
  Who has access to the budget to pay for help?—the departmental manager

It is clear therefore that although the training adviser's point of contact was originally the personnel and training manager, the complete client system is much wider. Given the number of times the departmental manager appears in the answers, the adviser would be foolhardy to go ahead with the assignment without involving her directly in the contracting process. Equally, to go ahead without considering the work group would be foolish as they are the only part of the client system who can actually do something about the problem. In this example the contracting process has become a good deal more complicated than a simple conversation with the training manager. Indeed, it appears that that individual is only a small part of the client system.

We would argue that this sort of situation is common for many internal consultants, in many different organizational settings and in all kinds of specialist fields throughout industry, commerce, national and local government, education and voluntary groups. Great care is therefore needed to ensure that before you get very far into your intervention you have identified (as far as you can) all the parts of the client system. Also, as far as possible, you will need to work with all these various parts of the system so that you don't get to the end and find that the implementation doesn't go ahead because you didn't identify who had to authorize the necessary finance.

The internal consultant

If you are to be a consultant you have to have a client who needs your help with a problem or difficulty. External consultants are usually there by invitation, but this may not be so for the internal consultant. As an internal consultant you may be imposed by the client's boss or by someone who recognizes that there is a problem and has the authority to order a consultation to take place. This is likely to give rise to all manner of difficulties when you are trying to establish a relationship or find out what the client's needs are. The following appear to us to be some of the advantages and disadvantages we experienced when working as internal consultants:

Advantages	Disadvantages
You may be able to take longer gaining entry	You are part of the culture you are seeking to change
You will probably know the client	Your department may have a poor image
You may know something about the client's problems	You may have a poor image
You know the history of the company	You may be imposed by the organization
You may share the same values	You may know things about the client that you can't disclose
You may spot non-genuine reasons for calling you in	You may have problems over confidentiality
You will probably know where to go for more information	You may be part of the problem
You will be able to find the real client more easily	You may have difficulty consulting either above you or below you in grade or status
You may already have established a good reputation for helping	You may have to confront people who might take offence
You may be able to ask for help from other internal consultants	You may be discounted as a prophet in your own land
You may find it easier to get involved in implementation and follow-up	You may fear that giving bad news could adversely affect your career prospects

We have found that many of these disadvantages exist solely in the mind of the internal consultant and are not borne out in practice. However, it is our view that if any of them appear to be potential disadvantages they are best highlighted as early in the consultation as possible.

The consulting cycle

Whenever you decide to work with someone to help solve a problem you are beginning a process which is similar to starting a journey together. The journey starts with an initial meeting and hopefully ends with the implementation of a different and more effective way of operating. The phases that make up this consulting cycle are:

1 Starting the consultation—making initial contact and establishing a working relationship (or, as we call it, gaining entry).
2 Contracting—finding out what the client wants.
3 Collecting data—finding out what happens now.
4 Making sense of the data—diagnosing the problem.
5 Generating options, making decisions and planning.
6 Implementing the plans and taking action.
7 Disengaging—arranging any necessary follow-up action.

This presents you with your first dilemma as a consultant. More often than not your client will want to tell you all about the problem and what needs to be done about it at the very first meeting. You, on the other hand, will know the folly of rushing into data collection and problem solving without getting to know your client, letting the client get to know you and reaching clear agreement on what he or she wants you to do, i.e. contracting.

This is likely to be even more difficult for the internal consultant. The temptation to gloss over these early phases is likely to be very strong as you will often be expected to know quite a lot about your potential clients and their problems. Before going any further, perhaps we should give a brief overview of each of the phases in our model of the consulting cycle.

Starting the consultation This consists of making initial contact with the client and starting to build a relationship—we call it gaining entry. Initial contact in this context means the first meeting with a person you assume to be the client. This may not always be the case but until you gain sufficient entry you will probably not find out one way or the other. To prepare for this meeting you will need to have given some thought to how you feel. Are you ready for the meeting? Are you as well prepared as you might be? What sort of first impression do you want to make? Are you in the right frame of mind to meet your client and deal with any difficulties that might arise?

Gaining entry means you and the client coming together to start to build a relationship of mutual trust and respect. You will want to find out a little about the client and the situation the client is in, as well as getting to know something about the problem you are there to help solve. You will also want the client to find out something about you so that confidence in you can begin to build up.

Contracting Contracting is about making explicit as many of the client's needs as you can. It is also the opportunity to let the client know, as explicitly as possible, what you are prepared to do and what part you want the client to play in the problem-solving process. It is important for both of you to understand in detail your mutual expectations of the relationship—who will do what and any boundaries that may exist. Contracting is therefore about ownership. One of the main difficulties in contracting is deciding when you have done enough to begin working on the problem. Delay too long and your client is likely to get frustrated with your apparent inactivity. Cut it short and you may find that your mutual expectations have not been specific enough and that too much is left to the imagination. In the context of client-centred consulting, contracting is not an exact science and there are bound to be grey areas. Fortunately, you can usually renegotiate as you progress through the assignment.

Collecting data This means collecting data about what is happening now. Provided you have completed gaining entry and contracting satisfactorily you should have a clear idea of where the client's difficulty lies. You will then be able to help the client collect data relevant to the problem. There are many sources for this data: factual data from staff or records; feelings and opinions of everyone involved or comments and attitudes of both internal and external customers. Most professions have their own methods of collecting the data they need. So whether you are a work study engineer, an operational research scientist, an auditor, a safety adviser or a personnel officer you will know what data you need to help you in your particular specialist field. However, apart from that, you will also be collecting data that gives you an impression of how the problem is managed, what organizational constraints are in place, what policies and procedures help or hinder how the department operates. And even as you collect this sort of organizational data you will have feelings about the staff, the managers and the environment which come to you through your intuition. All this data can be useful and can be fed back to the client.

Up to now the phases in the consulting cycle have been linear, following each other in a sequence as shown in Figure 1.2. While it is often necessary to go back and forth from one to another it is generally possible to complete one before going on to the next. But by the time you reach the point where you begin to help the client collect data, the cyclical part of consulting has begun.

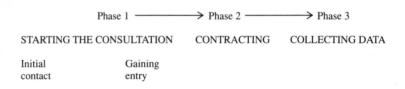

Phase 1 ⟶ Phase 2 ⟶ Phase 3

STARTING THE CONSULTATION   CONTRACTING   COLLECTING DATA

Initial   Gaining
contact   entry

Figure 1.2 *The first three phases of consultation*

Making sense of the data and diagnosing the problem

This phase of the cycle (see Figure 1.3) involves helping the client to spend time reflecting, questioning and discussing the data in order to make sense of it in terms of the difficulty being faced. Where there is insufficient data you may have to return to the previous phase and collect some more; where there is sufficient data or too much data, you may have to help the client determine what is important and relevant. In this case the data may need sorting or presenting in a clearer, more understandable way. It may be possible for you to offer the client data-presentation frameworks such as critical path analysis to help the client decide what extra data is needed. Alternatively, you could help by designing a questionnaire or actually collecting the data yourself. But whatever way you choose to help, the decision about which data or information to collect must come from the client.

This phase presents another significant dilemma for the client-centred consultant. On the one hand, you want to stay with the client's diagnosis so that you don't take ownership of the problem. But on the other hand you will often realize that the client is dealing with symptoms rather

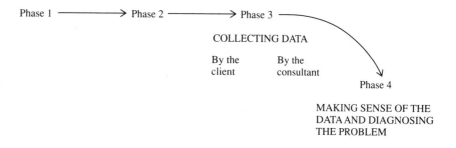

Figure 1.3   The fourth phase added

than the real problem. Often the client will stay firmly in the content or task aspects of the problem when the real difficulties are embedded in issues about how the problem is managed and how people feel about it. This issue about the real problem may have to be confronted before the client enters the next phase.

Generating options, making decisions and planning

Once the problem has been diagnosed you should be in a position to help your client generate the maximum number of options or possible solutions. In client-centred consulting it sometimes happens that you can see more options then the client can. Great care has to be taken about introducing these options, or the client may adopt one without really thinking and then blame you when it doesn't solve the problem. So in many situations it is better to stick with the client's chosen option even though you can think of a 'better' one. Your job is to challenge and confront so that your client doesn't just take the easy option. You may also have to help your client think through the implications of the decisions he or she makes so that there is as little doubt as possible that the right decision has been made.

Having made the decision the next step involves planning. Without a detailed plan of action very little is likely to happen to solve the problem. It is your job to encourage the client to question every aspect of the plan, to try to foresee what might go wrong and to anticipate the resources required (including time and financial costs). You are also there to help the client get commitment from the whole client system before implementation.

Helping the client in Phases 4 and 5 might involve introducing some theory to the client (see Figure 1.4). Such theory might help to make sense of the data, or diagnose the problem, or it might help to make decisions or plans. The kind of theory that might be of use could be just those theories you use to help yourself. This brings in yet another dilemma for the client-centred consultant. Do you merely use the theory to help the client, or do you spend time *teaching* the theory so that the client will be able to use it to solve similar problems in the future without assistance?

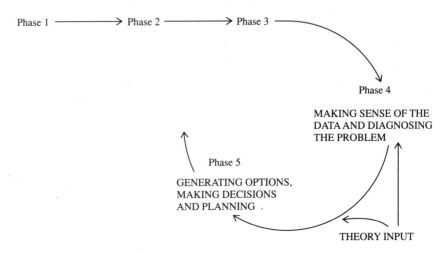

Phase 1 ——————→ Phase 2 ——————→ Phase 3

Phase 4

MAKING SENSE OF THE
DATA AND DIAGNOSING
THE PROBLEM

Phase 5

GENERATING OPTIONS,
MAKING DECISIONS
AND PLANNING

THEORY INPUT

Figure 1.4   The fifth phase added

**Implementing the
plan and taking
action**

Many consultants leave before the plans are implemented and action taken. They will often write a report recommending certain action and present it to the client either by post or at a feedback meeting. Sometimes they will then be told 'leave it with us' or 'thank you, that's really helpful—we will let you know what happens'. What you really know is that that is likely to be the last anyone hears about the report or its recommendations. The only way you can be sure that the plan is implemented is to be there while it happens. You may agree to be part of the implementation team but not to be in charge. Your job is to be there monitoring, mentoring, encouraging, supporting, confronting, opening doors or counselling and training, but not to take ownership. It may be very tempting to take a leading role during implementation especially if you think there is a danger of all your hard work being wasted. We always try to remember that the problem belongs to the client and so does the solution. If clients wish to exercise the option to do nothing, that is their privilege. Figure 1.5 shows how Phase 6 completes the cyclical part of consulting.

In our experience most barriers to implementation are about four key issues: capability, organization, ownership and leadership. Briefly, this means that people do not have the skills and knowledge needed, or believe that they don't. They may not be really committed to the plan either because they were not involved or because their attitude to the problem and its solution is one of apathy or mistrust, and therefore there is no ownership. Alternatively, the leadership may be such that people do not believe that the organization or its managers are committed and fear they will not provide the support necessary for the solution to work. Equally, where people involved in the implementation come from different disciplines, how they are organized can become a problem. Unless these issues are addressed during the planning stage, successful implementation is highly problematic.

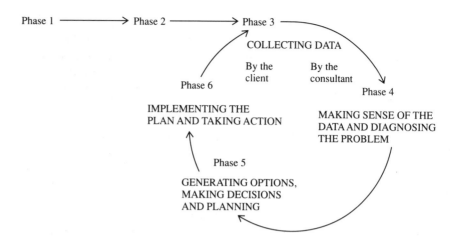

Figure 1.5 *The sixth phase added*

Disengaging   Once the plans have been implemented and action taken it is necessary to check that the new way of working is what is required and has replaced the old way which was causing the problem. If it has then you can probably disengage with some certainty that the new way of operating will stay in place. If it hasn't then you may have to go around the consulting cycle again until it does. You may have to help the clients examine the options or generate more. You may have to help them make different decisions or amend their plans. You may have to go further back into the process to examine the data, make different inferences from it and amend the diagnosis. You may even have to go back to collect more data or revisit the contract to check whether or not it contributed to inadequate implementation. Figure 1.6 shows the position of disengagement in the consulting process.

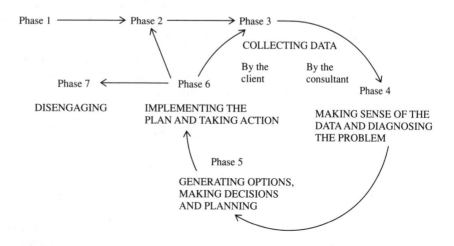

Figure 1.6 *The seventh phase added*

However, and whenever, you disengage it is vitally important that you do it well. Your aim should be to bring the consultation to a satisfactory end for both the client and yourself. It is especially important for the internal consultant to leave on good terms with the client, however successful or unsuccessful the outcome of the consultation. Your reputation and that of your colleagues in your department may well depend on how well you disengage. We were reminded of this recently by a colleague who had omitted to disengage from a project because the project leader was someone she saw every day on the same floor of the same building in which they both worked. She was roundly chastized by the project leader on the Monday following the Friday on which the project ended. 'You never came to say goodbye,' he complained. 'It would have been nice to celebrate what we had achieved.' For those of you who find endings of any sort hard, remember that your client may find them equally difficult.

Follow-up

Follow-up may often be needed to help the client maintain the implementation to the required standard. It may be that you have to arrange monitoring and support for the client either in the short term or on a continuous or occasional basis. However, it is very easy to get seduced into being available long after you should have left the client alone. Client dependency is easy to develop but very hard to stop. If your follow-up action happens some time after the implementation you may well find yourself having to start a new consultation from initial contact and gaining entry.

The following chapters of the book will examine each of these phases in detail in order to equip you to carry out more successful consulting assignments.

Learning styles and the consulting process

Understanding your learning style is likely to help considerably in increasing your learning power and will enable you to get the most from your interventions as a consultant. It will also help you understand the learning strengths of your clients and therefore their abilities in the various stages of the consulting cycle.

We have, for many years, helped our clients to see the relevance of their learning styles and their applicability to their problem-solving and consulting ability. In this respect we have been greatly influenced by Kolb (1981, 1985) and believe it is worth while spending some time assimilating his ideas. Basically Kolb argues that there are four distinct stages in the learning cycle, as shown in Figure 1.7.

Learning from feeling	Learning from specific experiences
	Relating to people
	Sensitivity to feelings and people
Learning by watching	Careful observation before making a judgement
	Viewing things from different perspectives
	Looking for the meaning of things

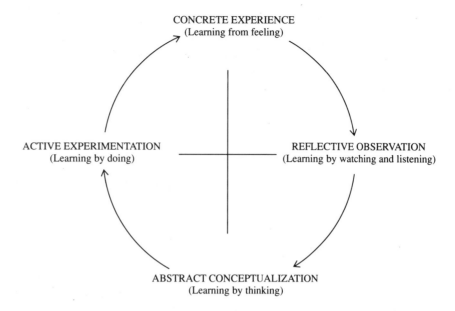

CONCRETE EXPERIENCE
(Learning from feeling)

ACTIVE EXPERIMENTATION
(Learning by doing)

REFLECTIVE OBSERVATION
(Learning by watching and listening)

ABSTRACT CONCEPTUALIZATION
(Learning by thinking)

Figure 1.7   Kolb learning styles
Source: David Kolb, *Learning Style Inventory*, McBer & Company, 1985. This
material may not be reproduced in any way, except with the written permission
of McBer & Company, 137 Newbury Street, Boston, MA 02116, USA (617) 437-
7080.

Learning by thinking	Logical analysis of ideas
	Systematic planning
	Acting on intellectual understanding of a situation
Learning by doing	Ability to get things done
	Risk taking
	Influencing people and events through action

From these descriptions you will realize that no one style fits you completely. This is because each person's learning style is a combination of
the four basic styles. However, most people have one or more styles
they are comfortable with and this may well distort their ability to learn
and also tend to pull them towards particular phases of the consulting
cycle. Combinations of the four basic descriptions provide the styles
described below.

Combining *concrete experience* with *reflective observation* generates a style
called *diverger*:

• Sees concrete situations from many points of view
• Understands people and is sensitive to feelings
• Recognizes problems but observes rather than takes action
• Open-minded, adaptable to change, lots of imagination

Combining *reflective observation* with *abstract conceptualization* generates a
style called *assimilator*:

- Collects and understands a wide range of information
- Puts information into concise, logical form
- Focuses on abstract ideas and concepts rather than people
- Logical soundness more important than practicality
- Creates models and plans and develops theories

Combining *abstract conceptualization* with *active experimentation* generates a style called *converger*:

- Finds practical uses for theories and ideas
- Able to solve problems and make decisions based on finding solutions
- Better with technical problems than interpersonal issues
- Deductive reasoning

Combining *active experimentation* with *concrete experience* generates a style called *accommodator*:

- Implements plans involving new challenges
- Acts more on intuition than logical analysis
- Relies on people rather than technical analysis for information
- Risk taking

Figure 1.8 illustrates how these styles fit into the basic model.

Those of you who have studied learning styles using the Honey and Mumford typology (1986) will recognize the similarity with those of Kolb.

Kolb	*Honey and Mumford*[1]
diverger	reflector
assimilator	theorist
converger	pragmatist
accommodator	activist

When the learning styles model is integrated with the consulting cycle it can be seen that some learning styles have particular strengths which are useful in particular phases of the consulting cycle (see Figure 1.9).

When collecting data about what is happening now the *accommodators* and *divergers* will be particularly useful. As you move into making sense of the data and diagnosing the problem you will want to make use of the *divergers* and *assimilators*. As you progress towards exploring options, making decisions and planning, the strengths of the *assimilators* are likely to be supplemented by those of the *convergers*, who are likely to be good at assessing the practicality of the solutions. The *convergers* will need the strengths of the *accommodators* when it comes to implementation. Your own learning style as a consultant is likely to attract you to certain phases of the consulting cycle so it is particularly important that you know what it is and do not hurry through the phases which don't fit with your preferred style. For example, it is likely to be hard for the very pragmatic consultant to keep the client working on making sense of the data and diagnosing the problem if all the time you are keen to get into implementation.

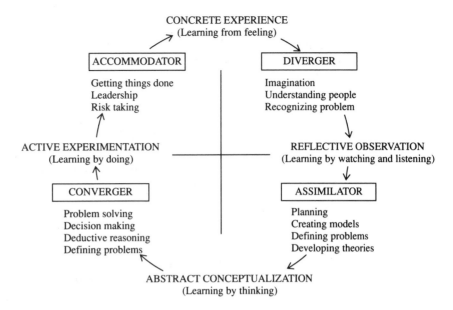

Figure 1.8 *Kolb learning styles*
Reproduced by permission of McBer & Company

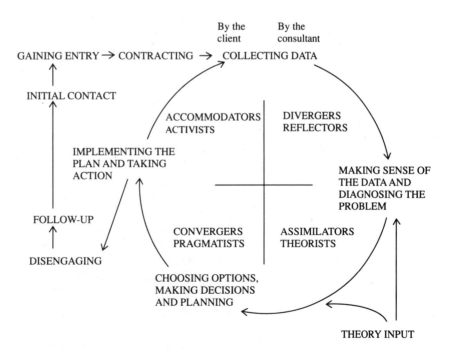

Figure 1.9 *Learning styles and the consulting process*

Similarly, if you like generating new ideas and recognizing problems but are not really concerned about putting them to work, you are likely to generate a great deal of frustration in a client who wants action rather than mature reflection.

Intervention styles

Intervention style is the term used to describe the behaviours that we adopt in our interactions with clients during our journey round the consulting cycle. Most of us have a particular style we are comfortable with when helping clients. However, if we have only one favourite style to use there are likely to be situations when that style is not effective enough. For instance, consultants in many professions are used to diagnosing clients' problems and prescribing the answers. In many situations where the consultant is the expert and the client is willing and able to take the prescription, the style is appropriate. But there are other equally effective styles available which are essential for the client-centred consultant. There is no part of the consulting process where one or more styles are not appropriate. The main point is that, whatever style you choose, there are consequences and implications. Furthermore, some styles are more important in some situations than others.

It is our experience that consulting styles are rarely even considered, so comfortable are we with our present style. Before looking at the alternative intervention styles available you may like to reflect on your own style preference. Imagine that you have a free choice about the kind of help you give to clients. Rank order the following statements to reflect how you prefer to work. Use 1 for your first choice through to 4 for your least preferred choice.

Ranking

A   I prefer to work with clients by helping them talk through or sort out how they feel about the problem.   ....

B   I prefer to work with clients by helping them gather and sift through information about the problem to help them define the situation more clearly and decide what to do.   ....

C   I prefer to work with clients by identifying and highlighting hidden or buried values and attitudes which may be having a disruptive effect on client behaviour or exacerbating the problem.   ....

D   I prefer to help clients by carefully examining the situation and then providing answers or solutions that will solve the problem and increase client effectiveness.   ....

Following Blake and Mouton's descriptions (1976, 1983) we would distinguish four distinct intervention styles which can be employed in different situations: *acceptant, catalytic, confrontational* and *prescriptive*.

Acceptant style   A consultant working in an acceptant style helps clients by empathic listening and by providing emotional support. This style of neutral, non-judgemental support can help clients to relax their defences, confront disabling emotional reactions and find their own way forward. It allows and encourages clients to clear what is blocking their ability to deal logically and rationally with their problem. In many respects it is typical of the early stages of counselling. However, as will be discussed later, it can also be useful in many other situations with individuals and groups.

Catalytic style   A consultant working in a catalytic style helps clients gather more data about the problem, sift through it to decide the relative importance of aspects of the data, or reflect upon it to make a diagnosis of the problem. Not all clients are short of information—some have so much that they can't see the wood for the trees. The intention behind the style is that once the clients have obtained and made sense of the data or information they will be able to choose options and move forward to solving the problem. Although the catalytic style can involve many types of data-gathering methodologies, it is perhaps typified at the interpersonal level by questions which begin with who, what, why, when, where and how. In this sense it is a diagnostic style. However, the important point is that, although catalytic interventions may help clients at the data-gathering stage, the solution is always generated by the clients themselves.

Confrontational style   A consultant working in a confrontational style helps the clients by calling attention to discrepancies between the values and beliefs they hold and how they put these values and beliefs into practice, i.e. their behaviour. Most of us have theories in our head (espoused theories) and yet we behave in ways which are quite contrary (theories in use). The confrontational style points out these differences to clients so that they are able to recognize the discrepancies and have an opportunity to decide if they wish to change.

Prescriptive style   Consultants working in a prescriptive style with clients generally listen to the clients' problem, collect the data they require, make sense of it from their own experience and present the clients with a solution or recommendations. It is probably the most common style used by specialists although it may not be the most effective. Typically, it is the style used by experts or those who think they are experts, e.g. doctors with their patients. The assumption is that the clients do not have the skill, knowledge or objectivity to make an accurate diagnosis or prescription of their own. Unfortunately, this is seldom the case; clients seldom know absolutely nothing about their problem and may have had the particular problem for some time. However, consultants can still use their expertise and experience by becoming a source of data to enable clients to provide their own solution or satisfactory way forward, without removing all freedom of action from the clients. As will be discussed later, there are situations in which the prescriptive style is entirely appropriate.

From our experience we would support Blake and Mouton and suggest that these four styles constitute a practical and comprehensive description of most legitimate consultant behaviour. However, despite the fact that all the styles can be of value, you will probably feel more comfortable with one or two (as the ranking exercise may have shown). You may also tend to use your preferred style more often than the others. This could be detrimental to the consultant/client relationship as all styles have their uses in different situations and phases of the consulting cycle. The key is being able to recognize when a particular style is needed and then to use it appropriately. To do this effectively you will need to know more about the behaviour associated with each style, the assumptions behind them, their uses, and the associated risks for the client and consultant. These are all covered in the Chapter 2 on Intervention Styles.

You may like to turn back and have a second look at your ranking now that you have read about each style. Assuming you have a good understanding of how you operate with clients it could provide insight into your favourite styles and highlight areas where you may need to do some additional work to become more client-centred.

Summary

- Consulting is what happens when one person has a problem or difficulty and seeks help from someone with special skills.
- Typically, counselling is a specialized type of consultancy and may form part of consulting.
- Consulting skills are needed by many specialists, advisers and helpers in organizations. Many managers are also beginning to find they need consulting skills.
- Consultants can be defined as those who find themselves having to influence or advise others without any formal authority or choosing not to use what authority they have.
- Client-centred consultants recognize that being sensitive and responsive to the needs of clients is as important as technical competence.
- The training role, used appropriately, can offer many opportunities for client-centred work.
- Clients can be single individuals, a disparate group or a whole organization. In organizations, it is often more practical to conceive of 'client systems'.
- The real client is defined by:
  - Who knows?
  - Who cares?
  - Who can?
- The consulting cycle follows the path:
  - Initial contact and gaining entry
  - Contracting
  - Collecting data
  - Making sense of the data—diagnosing the problem
  - Generating options, making decisions, planning
  - Implementing plans and taking action
  - Disengaging and follow-up

- The phases of consulting, from collecting data to implementation, form a cyclic path and are consistent with current thinking on experiential learning. Indeed, consulting and experiential learning are identical.
- The process of consulting requires a variety of personal styles. These are:
  - acceptant
  - catalytic
  - confrontational
  - prescriptive
- Being able to recognize and use all styles is an important element of consultant competence.

Checklist 1.1   *Your client-centredness as a consultant*

The following checklist is designed for you to assess the degree to which you feel client-centred in your work as a consultant, or how client-centred you think you would be if you are intending to work as an internal consultant.

Estimate your score before you complete the checklist by placing a cross where you think you will be on the following scale.

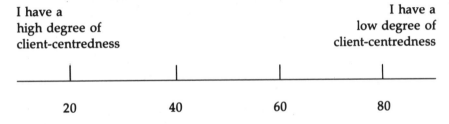

I have a high degree of client-centredness			I have a low degree of client-centredness
20	40	60	80

Now complete the checklist as honestly as you can. Try to get in touch with your *feelings* about each statement rather than scoring what you *think*.

Tick whichever column best represents your *feeling*

	I never feel this way	*I seldom feel this way*	*I often feel this way*	*I always feel this way*
1 I should be able to understand my client's problems as well as they do.	....	....	....	....
2 When I am giving advice and suggestions I really feel I am helping my clients.	....	....	....	....
3 I get defensive when challenged or confronted on something I feel strongly about.	....	....	....	....

	I never feel this way	I seldom feel this way	I often feel this way	I always feel this way
4 My self-esteem depends upon my being seen and acknowledged as expert in my field.	....	....	....	....
5 I like influencing my clients' behaviour by telling them what to do for the best.	....	....	....	....
6 I believe that my clients are generally not competent and skilful at problem solving.	....	....	....	....
7 I have a lot of experience and therefore I know the answers to most of my clients' problems.	....	....	....	....
8 I feel rejected as a person when people don't like what I do or say.	....	....	....	....
9 I don't like feedback which is negative, unconstructive or against my self-image.	....	....	....	....
10 I enjoy showing how clever I am by being witty and scoring points off people.	....	....	....	....
11 I find it hard to ask for help for myself.	....	....	....	....
12 I believe that most of my clients want me to solve their problems for them.	....	....	....	....
13 It is important for me to get the credit when my clients solve their problems with my help.	....	....	....	....
14 I know better than my clients what to do to solve their problems.	....	....	....	....
15 The only rationale for my being a consultant is to solve my clients' problems for them.	....	....	....	....
16 I like being in control when helping clients to solve problems.	....	....	....	....

	I never feel this way	I seldom feel this way	I often feel this way	I always feel this way
17 I do not believe that most of my clients want to solve their own problems.	....	....	....	....
18 If I have spent years getting my expertise it is a waste not to use it to solve problems for my clients.	....	....	....	....
19 I enjoy having clients who come to me with problems they cannot solve.	....	....	....	....
20 If clients ask me for advice I believe I should give it to them if I can.	....	....	....	....

Score 1 for each answer in the Never column
    2   Seldom
    3   Often
    4   Always

Total your score and transfer it to the client-centredness scale above.

Total [ ]

Rationale The classification of the items in the checklist is not a definitive one and some statements apply to more than one area. Generally, however, we have included statements which seek your feelings about being an expert/advice giver, your attitude to your clients and your self-image.

Expert/Advice giver: Items 1, 2, 4, 7, 14, 15, 16, 18, 20.
Attitude to clients: Items 5, 6, 10, 12, 14, 16, 17, 19.
Your self-image: Items 1, 2, 3, 4, 5, 8, 9, 10, 11, 13, 18.

If you found yourself ticking most of the *Often* and *Always* boxes and your score is above 50 you may have some difficulty in working in a client-centred way.

If you found yourself ticking most of the *Never* and *Seldom* boxes and your score is below 50 you may find it somewhat easier to work in a client-centred way.

To find out what you need to work on to become more client-centred, circle the item numbers above for all those items where you scored three or four. The pattern which emerges will indicate whether your blockages lie in being an expert/advice giver, your attitude to clients or your self-image. The rationale which follows may give you some indication of the areas to work on.

If your personal power does not depend upon your being seen as an expert,
If you have little desire to be in control,
If you do not automatically operate as a giver of advice,
If you are not concerned to influence other people's behaviour,
If you value yourself and value your clients even though they need your help,
If you have a positive self-image and can handle negative feedback, *then* you are likely to be working in a client-centred way already or you are likely to have little difficulty working in a client-centred way in future.

Note

[1] It is important to stress that our comparison of the learning styles used by Kolb and Honey and Mumford is not strictly accurate. Both sets of researchers base their work on the circular pattern of learning and at the general level their descriptions of the styles appear to have much in common. However, Honey and Mumford have built their views of the styles around recognizable statements of managerial behaviour. This has meant that their descriptions of learning styles are, in their view, more detailed than, and differ from, their apparent Kolb equivalents. Suffice to say that we have found that managers readily relate to the Kolb Learning Style Inventory and can use it to find ways of improving the effectiveness of their learning. However, we acknowledge the important contribution which Peter Honey and Alan Mumford have made to the current knowledge about how people learn and how they might become more effective learners, and the influence they have had on our own thinking.

2 Intervention styles

What is an intervention style?

As we saw in Chapter 1, intervention style is simply the name or label which describes our behaviour during interactions with clients.

Unfortunately, consultant style is often not even thought about, it is taken for granted as normal behaviour. Nevertheless, as consultants, whatever name we give to our normal automatic behaviour, it does have consequences for the clients. Take for example the advice-giving or prescriptive style. Traditionally, many types of specialist consultants have used this model of helping—indeed in some circumstances it can be very helpful. But as doctors are becoming increasingly aware, very often patients don't take the prescription or do not heed the advice. One of the difficulties with prescribing is that it takes from the clients any involvement or control, effectively leaving them impotent. The only choice they are left with is either to accept or reject the prescription. Also, style is a statement about how the consultant perceives helping. Prescribing implies that the clients cannot solve their own problems and/or that the prescriber is in possession of expert knowledge and knows a solution to the clients' problems. These are quite far-reaching implications and not always the case. As a consequence, many consultants are beginning to look at other styles of helping which can prove more effective.

Before looking at the styles available it is worth emphasizing that style affects the entire consulting relationship from initial contact to disengagement. There is no part of the relationship where you do not employ one or more intervention styles. The main point is that, whatever style you choose, it does have consequences. Furthermore, some styles are more important in some situations than in others.

As outlined in Chapter 1, we believe there are four distinct intervention styles which you can employ when working with clients. These are:

- acceptant
- catalytic
- confrontational
- prescriptive

These categories are similar to those described by Blake and Mouton in their book *Consultation: A Handbook for Individual and Organization Development* (1976, revised 1983). However, we have added many refinements and explanations to their original work and we have also deleted Blake and Mouton's fifth style category 'Theories and Principles', as we believe this is not an intervention style but more an intervention strategy. As such it is a way of combining the previous styles in a strategic manner while using theories, models and frameworks to help clients make more effective use of the data. Our simplified model therefore embraces only four distinct styles of approach.

From our experience of working with many client systems, we would argue that these four styles constitute a practical description of most legitimate consultant behaviour. However, it is worth while emphasizing again that, despite the fact that all of them can be of value, you will probably feel more comfortable with one or two (as the ranking exercise in Chapter 1 may have indicated). Unfortunately, you may also tend to employ your preferred styles more often than the others. This could be detrimental to the consulting relationship as all styles have their uses in different situations. They key is being able to recognize when a particular style is needed and then using it appropriately. To do this effectively we need to know a great deal more about the behaviour, uses, risks and assumptions embodied in each of the styles. The following sections in this chapter examine each style in detail.

Acceptant intervention style

On the surface acceptant interventions appear easy—they merely involve listening. Yet in practice this is rarely the case. An effective acceptant approach involves a highly sophisticated set of interpersonal skills. In principle this means setting aside one's own view of a problem or difficulty and instead attempting to understand it from the client's viewpoint. This ability is perhaps best summarized by the expression 'being able to feel how the other person's shoes pinch'. In essence it is about accepting the client, 'warts and all'.

Acceptant interventions are characterized by the skills of empathic understanding which, in many respects, are congruent with skills used in the early stages of client-centred counselling. They encourage and permit the client to address, disclose and discuss thoughts and feelings which would remain repressed with other intervention styles.

Virtually every problem, difficulty or change we experience in life is accompanied by some form of emotional response. This is a natural and normal human reaction. Sometimes these emotions or feelings are uninvited and unwanted—nevertheless they exist. Where they persist they may disrupt normal objective behaviour and make it difficult for us to continue with everyday activities and deny us the ability to function normally. It is also worth noting that feelings which disrupt objectivity need not necessarily be negative; for example, euphoria can lead to unbalanced judgements or decisions just as easily as anger or despair. Imagine the problems and difficulties resulting from love at first sight!

Individuals or groups who are able to function objectively are not influenced by disabling feelings that warp their perspective on situations. Indeed, the ability to perceive situations or problems objectively is an essential first step in tackling cyclical or habitual behaviour. For example, a member of staff who has been transferred to a new department, working for a new manager he dislikes, may be so angry at the change that he may be unable to function in a job which should be well within his normal capacities. Alternatively, the woman who is made redundant may have reached such a low level of self-esteem that she is no longer able to project her abilities in new job applications or at interview. A third common example is the individual who is so overwhelmed with private or domestic problems that he can no longer function at work. The list is endless.

Problems, difficulties and change affect everyone emotionally and sometimes this can skew the ability to think and act rationally. This is as true for issues at work as it is elsewhere in life (and occasionally one can have a 'knock-on' effect into the other—problems at work can affect domestic life and vice versa).

The first stage in helping involves recognizing and acknowledging the feelings that exist. These may be feelings about the situation, feelings about the problem, or feelings about self or others. Only by expressing and working through disruptive feelings can the client begin to make progress. Sometimes these feelings are quite mild whereas on other occasions they may be overwhelming, so they may take proportionally shorter or longer lengths of time to work through. Similarly, different individuals will take varying lengths of time to come to terms with the same change simply because of individual differences and different personal circumstances—there are no hard and fast rules. However, working through the feeling content of any problem is an essential prerequisite to problem solving.

Sometimes, in a purely acceptant approach, helping clients work through the feelings is all the help that is needed. Having recognized and worked on the feelings, clients have sufficient resources of their own to engage in problem solving and find their own way forward. On other occasions some other intervention style may also be needed. But when changing style you must be sure this is to meet genuine client needs rather than your own style preference.

It is also worth remembering that assisting clients might involve helping them to accept some negative event in life. Not all the difficulties or changes that people experience have nice neat solutions. The most obvious examples of this are with 'life crisis' problems such as bereavement, debilitating illness, or serious sensory or motor impairment. However, situations also arise in the work setting which cannot be resolved (in the sense of everything being put back to normal), for example, where skills or roles have become redundant or disappeared, or where new automated systems have replaced older manual systems. Staff may long for everything to be put back as it was, but this is no longer an option. The 'solution' lies in their accepting and coming to terms with the change and then learning some new skills or finding new roles. There is also little doubt that negotiating these kinds of transitions in life is undertaken more easily with the benefit of skilled help. In this respect, when you are able to use the acceptant style effectively, you become one of the client's most powerful allies.

Underlying assumptions

Acceptant interventions are underpinned by a few important assumptions. The first is that the clients are impaired or disabled from coming to terms with the problem or cannot find a way forward because of their feelings. It is assumed that the feelings prevent the clients from carrying out any effective problem solving or decision making to help resolve the issue. The principal form of help which the acceptant style conveys is to give clients an opportunity to discuss and work through or come to terms with how they feel. If carried out effectively, acceptant interventions will address the feelings and enable clients to diagnose and resolve their own situation more objectively.

A second implicit assumption is that clients have sufficient resources to find their own way forward once the feelings have been acknowledged and resolved. Your role is principally to help and support your clients while they address the way they feel. This is radically different from most interpretations of helping. Conventionally, helping is construed as giving more direct assistance in the form of opinion, advice or suggestion. These forms of helping are the antithesis of acceptant interventions. Under an acceptant approach clients are helped to find their own way forward without external prompting.

Obviously, if a pure acceptant approach is to be of value, these assumptions must be appropriate. Where they are not, you will generally need to use other styles in combination with acceptant interventions. However, as will be discussed later, the acceptant style can be of value at all stages of an assignment.

How do I use an acceptant style?

With acceptant interventions your aim is to provide clients with emotional and personal security such that they can work through their difficulties and generate their own set of actions. However, a common misconception is that when you use an acceptant approach you act like a 'nodding donkey': that is, you simply listen passively and accept all that clients say. We must emphasize that this is not the case. Effective acceptant interventions involve a wide range of behaviour, including:

- Adopting an open, non-threatening body posture;
- Using direct non-oppressive eye contact;
- Smiling and nodding acceptance of clients' descriptions of their situation;
- Using positive para-verbal signals such as 'uh-huh-' to encourage clients to say more;
- Attempting to understand the problem or difficulty from the clients' point of view and communicating this understanding by restating, paraphrasing or summarizing the clients' description of the situation;
- Encouraging clients to say more by using statements such as 'tell me more . . .' and then confirming understanding;
- Encouraging clients to express both their thoughts and (often more importantly) their feelings about the situation. If necessary using direct questions like:

– How do you feel about that?

– How do you feel?

– How did you feel in that situation?

- Picking up 'feeling' words which clients may have used and reflecting them back. In a sense, giving clients permission to explore feelings further if they wish;
- Listening when clients use descriptive phrases that mask feelings and giving them the opportunity to explore the feelings further if they wish. For example, clients may use phrases like:

  – 'Walking on a knife edge'

  – 'Hanging in mid air'

  – 'Being used like a doormat'

  – 'Walking on eggshells'

  – 'Feeling like the filling in a sandwich'

  It is therefore important to ask:

  – How does it feel to be hanging in mid air?

  – How does it feel walking on a knife edge?

  – How does it feel hanging in mid air?

  – How does it feel being used like a doormat?

  – How does it feel walking on eggshells?

  – How does it feel to feel like the filling in a sandwich?

  All of these (and many others) are expressions which could hide a raft of much deeper feelings that merit further exploration;
- Picking up how clients might feel as they describe their situation and tentatively suggesting how they might feel;
- Using all data brought by the clients, their words, their body language, tone of voice, looks etc., and their behaviour with you;
- Using silence to allow clients time to think;
- Staying outside any discussion or value judgement concerning the 'content' of the clients' problem: neither agreeing nor disagreeing with what clients say and not taking sides;
- Accepting that clients' initial definition of the problem is not necessarily the real problem. However, working with this until clients feel sufficiently secure to disclose the real problem or clarify their thinking to a point where they can engage in redefining the problem more accurately. The acceptant style demands that all diagnoses are made by the clients.

The important point to note is that acceptant interventions involve much more than mere passive listening. Experienced practitioners attempt to listen at three levels; first, to what the clients are saying; second, to what clients are *not* saying; and third (perhaps the most difficult of all), to what clients cannot bring themselves to say. There is no question that this level of concentration is very demanding and requires considerable practice.

What risks are involved?

Preliminary exercise

Before reading the rest of this section you might like to generate your own list of possible risks for both consultant and client when using an acceptant approach.

Although the acceptant style is a very gentle way of working, there are several risks for both consultant and client. Blake and Mouton (1983) identify two:

- It is possible that clients, having acknowledged and worked through the emotional component of a problem, choose to accept the circumstances that caused the problem rather than take any action to initiate change. This could well be the case in instances where the amount of change needed appears overwhelming or too much to take on. As a consequence, clients could choose to remain locked in their existing cycle of behaviour.
- The second risk is perhaps more subtle. The acceptant style eases and gives permission for overt expression of feelings within the consulting relationship. It is possible that some clients may carry this permission into other settings and, in a sense, 'go public' in situations where such forms of emotional outburst are against the norms. As a consequence, they could meet hostility, resentment and rejection, perhaps making the situation even worse than at the outset.

Beyond these two we feel it is important to highlight a few other risks we have observed when working with many different client groups; these include:

- Situations where clients touch very powerful feelings of, for example, anger, sadness or despair, feelings so powerful that the consultant can become very uncomfortable and as a result inhibit any natural expression of feelings by the clients. It is essential to recognize that acceptant questions or statements create an atmosphere which permits open expression of feelings, sometimes very strong feelings. In our experience it is not unusual for clients to experience a whole range of powerful emotions when describing how they feel about their particular situation. A few tears or anger are not unusual in either human life or consultation, but it does not help if consultants use expressions like:
  - There's no need to cry.
  - Pull yourself together.
  - I'm sure it's not that bad.
  - Would you like a few minutes alone?
  - There's no need to get angry about it.
  Such expressions seek to meet the needs of the consultant rather than the clients. They inhibit further dialogue and effectively say to clients 'these feelings are not permitted'. From what we have seen previously, this is directly opposite to what we are trying to achieve with this style.
- Expression of feelings can also raise issues concerned with confidentiality. Clients who choose to recognize and acknowledge their feelings become more vulnerable as a result. They will be aware that the consultant knows a great deal more about them than anyone

else within the organization. This is particularly important for the internal consultant and can become a major problem if confidentiality is not strictly observed.

Finally, it is also worth noting that many consultants who are new to this method of working experience discomfort when they attempt to use an acceptant style. The traditional expectation of consulting is more active—the offering of suggestions or advice. From this perspective an acceptant intervention can feel passive. However, there is no doubt that when used effectively it becomes a very powerful intervention style which enables and empowers clients to generate their own solutions.

When can I use an acceptant style?

Acceptant interventions can be used throughout most consulting assignments. Feelings and emotions will always be present to some degree in all the phases of your relationship with a client. For example, during initial contact and gaining entry, you can use the acceptant style to:

- acknowledge how the client feels
- discuss any client resistance
- discuss any fight/flight reaction on the part of the client

During contracting you may encounter resistance if the client feels threatened in any way. Equally, during data gathering you could surface a client's feelings or even generate them. Decision making and implementation invariably involve some form of change and this could easily generate very strong feelings. Similarly, disengagement necessarily involves feelings of separation and loss. It follows, therefore, that the most appropriate style to help at all these points is acceptant. We have argued earlier that consultation is principally about change, and all change, whether large or small, technical or human, involves feelings. The issue for us as consultants is not whether there will be an emotional response, but how it will manifest itself. An acceptant approach is the only intervention style that will provide help when feelings and emotions are a component of the problem.

Acceptant style in practice

The first illustration summarizes an experience of one of our colleagues who is involved with helping organizations select, install and come to terms with computer systems. For us it is an interesting example as it highlights how technological change has important emotional repercussions for the people involved.

The particular client organization had recently installed a new computer system for dealing with customer accounts. The consultant was called in as a result of ongoing complaints by staff about perceived deficiencies in the system. After making contact and agreeing an outline contract with the departmental manager the consultant realized she would need to talk with the staff who used the system on a daily basis in order to get to the root of the problem. Initially, her intention was to use a diagnostic, catalytic approach to find out how the staff were using the system. However, it quickly became apparent that the staff were so uptight that their responses were skewed by strong feelings of antagonism towards both their management and the new system. In response, the consultant changed her style of approach to acceptant in order to help the group acknowledge and explore their feelings. It eventually emerged that group members were simply unsure how to use the system, but their lack of knowledge was masked by anger and resentment at having the system foisted on them when, in their view, the old manual system was perfectly sound. For the consultant, further work with the staff group was straightforward; once the feelings of resentment and loss had been worked through, it consisted primarily of helping them really to understand why the system was being introduced, helping them to accept the need and to adopt the system as their own. However, this was not the end of her work. To complete the assignment she needed to provide the management group who were responsible for introducing the new system with feedback on their method of introduction. This required yet another change of consulting style and proved to be the most demanding aspect of the whole project.

In retrospect the consultant recognized that the key to this assignment was her early switch to an acceptant style when working with the staff group. They were angry about the lack of consultation when the system was originally planned and clearly were in no mood to learn how to use the system once it was installed. However, for the consultant, what started as a technical assignment turned out to be one that was more concerned with human relations and management style.

A second illustration comes from our own work with companies who have found it necessary to carry out an outplacement exercise (a euphemism for redundancy). In such cases the early phases of the consultation, including initial contracting, are usually carried out with the appropriate management group within the client organization. However, the main focus of intervention is with those who are to be made redundant. Once the job losses have been announced (usually done without warning), we have attempted to make contact with the individuals or groups affected and tactfully offer our services. In virtually every case we have seen, it has been immediately apparent (from body language alone) that the self-esteem of these people has been shattered. The feelings of rejection and loss have often been overwhelming and as a consequence addressing the feelings has taken priority over any other concern.

The consulting style which seems most appropriate in such circumstances is acceptant and we have used this extensively during our early work with affected groups. Only when the feelings of rejection and loss have been acknowledged and addressed have we attempted to move on to more practical steps which could lead the individuals involved to new employment.

A final obvious illustration of an acceptant intervention will strike a chord with most training consultants. It involved a participant on a training course who touched deep unresolved feelings and reacted emotionally. The experience occurred while we were carrying out counselling training with a group of managers as part of a general management course. The particular case which the group were discussing concerned bereavement. However, the members of the group were not aware that one of them had very recently lost a close member of his family. This only became apparent to the others when his feelings became overwhelming and he started to cry. His immediate reaction was to attempt to leave the room and be on his own. Fortunately, one of the other group members (who was a skilled consultant) quickly pursued him and attempted to provide support. In effect this consisted of being with the grieving man and simply giving him space to talk. Obviously the most valuable consulting style to serve this end is acceptant. After a short while they were able to rejoin the main group and continue with the session. In retrospect the group was strengthened as a result of the experience; rather than merely discussing bereavement as an intellectual exercise, they were able to relate it to first-hand experience.

In conclusion, the acceptant style would be useful in:

- Helping individuals and groups deal with self-defeating reactions such as anger, hostility or frustration towards people in authority—managers, supervisors, parents, police, inspectors or teachers.
- Helping individuals and groups to release themselves from fear of the unknown consequences if they confront an authoritarian boss, admit a mistake, ask for help, confess to being under stress or lack confidence to do the job, in a culture where such a thing is seen as weakness.
- Helping individuals and groups explore, express and heal the negative feelings they have about each other, other groups, the system, equipment which fails, trade unions, management, suppliers or customers.
- Helping individuals and groups come to terms with disabling emotional reactions which may lead to discouragement or demotivation at work: demotion, refused promotion, lack of feedback, poor appraisal, lack of consultation or involvement.

Overall, acceptant interventions help people to unload troublesome thoughts, reactions and feelings and allow clients to be more objective about the situation they are in.

Summary

- Acceptant interventions attempt to convey an understanding of the problem or difficulty from the client's point of view.
- All problems and difficulties in life are accompanied by feelings. Sometimes these feelings distort our ability to make decisions.
- Acceptant helping involves recognizing and acknowledging feelings. It can be used throughout the consulting relationship but may feel uncomfortable for inexperienced consultants.
- Acceptant interventions may involve helping clients come to terms with negative life experiences.
- Acceptant interventions assume that:

- clients cannot decide what to do because feelings obstruct or distort their judgement.
- clients have sufficient resources to make their own decisions once the feelings have been acknowledged and resolved.
- Acceptant interventions employ behaviour which:
  - accepts and acknowledges the clients' perspective;
  - helps clients identify and explore their feelings;
  - gives clients space to talk without being judged.

Catalytic intervention style

Many years ago during chemistry lessons at school we were taught that a catalyst speeds up a chemical reaction but is not itself changed as a result of the reaction. By current standards this is probably a naive definition, but in consultation the concept of a catalytic style is meant to describe a method of interacting with clients which speeds up the rate of change taking place. In situations where this is appropriate clients usually do not have enough relevant data to make a decision about change or have so much data they are overwhelmed and can't distinguish the essentials. To move forward they need some form of catalyst to help them either to obtain more information, or to sort out the surfeit of information in order to make the decision manageable.

This may sound complicated and highly scientific but it can be a very simple process. For example, one of the authors recalls an instance when his parents could not decide whether to move to a new house. They had discussed the decision for several months, visited the new location, involved other family members, seeking their advice, but to everyone's dismay were unable to make a choice. The decision was finally laid to rest as a result of a simple catalytic intervention by the author concerned. In effect he sat down with the couple and helped them to list on a sheet of paper the advantages and disadvantages of moving and, on a second sheet of paper, the advantages and disadvantages of staying where they were. Once the information was rearranged in this form the decision became obvious. His parents chose to remain where they were and the issue never surfaced again.

This illustration encapsulates one type of catalytic intervention, where the consultant used a very simple model for shaping and presenting the clients' data. In this case the author simply helped the clients rearrange the information they had in such a way that it became meaningful and helpful. It is important to note that he did not add any information himself (by way of suggestions, opinions or advice), he simply helped the couple find a more effective way of looking at the information. Furthermore, as with the acceptant style, the actual decision was made by the clients. The author did not influence them in either direction.

Clearly, in any situation a whole range of data-analysis and presentation techniques is available; these could include:

- decision trees
- force field analysis
- critical path method

- cost benefit analysis
- flow charts
- bar charts and histograms

Some of these techniques are discussed in detail in Chapter 7 and all of them can be used as tools for catalytic interventions. However, the choice of which is most appropriate will depend on the circumstances surrounding a particular assignment together with the type of data to be presented.

In some cases this process of rearranging and presenting the data will highlight where there are significant gaps in the information available. The client may then need help to gather additional data. This could involve individual or group interviews, questionnaires, direct observation, document analysis, etc. All the data-gathering methods discussed in Chapter 6 could be usefully employed. An example of helping the client gather additional data occurred for us with an assignment where we were attempting to help a group develop its teamwork skills. It quickly became apparent that although group members were committed to the task they were struggling at a feelings level. We were able to surface this data by using a simple review questionnaire which each member completed at the end of the group meetings. The results were tabulated and shared among all group members, and time was set aside at each subsequent meeting for the group to carry out a similar review. This identified areas which the group needed to work on and helped them develop as a team.

Once again, the consultants added nothing other than a review period at the end of each meeting together with a simple technique for surfacing previously undisclosed data. Also, the decisions on which aspects of teamwork the group should tackle were made by the group members following their discussion of the data. However, this example is also important in respect of the type of data collected. In many settings data is regarded as physical—reality, facts or numbers. But here the data collected was different—it was information on how the group behaved and how individuals felt. Clearly, this is a much more exotic interpretation of data, but it was vital information which the group needed to address if they were to make progress and develop as a team. In the catalytic approach all kinds of data can be of value. This includes numerical and factual data but it also embraces feelings, hunches and behaviour.

It is also important to note that catalytic interventions start from the client's felt needs. Obviously, as consultants, we hope that by gathering and structuring the information the initial felt needs will be redefined during the consultation to enable the client to address real needs (but this is always a risk). For example, initial felt needs which may prompt a client to request help could include problems such as:

- low productivity
- poor product or service quality
- excessive machine down-time
- persistent late delivery

- high sickness absence rates
- rising costs
- decreasing profits

However, the real needs underlying these could include:

- inadequate supervisory or management skills
- poor relationships between departments
- unmotivated employees
- poor decision making
- inadequate information

Obviously, it is essential that the client's problem, real or felt, is eventually solved. But within the catalytic approach this means you must accept the client's definition at the outset (even though you may have a hunch that there is much more to the problem). As you help the client collect and shape the data on the felt problem the deeper issues are highly likely to emerge.

Although it is feasible that the client will not identify the real problem, the main advantage of a catalytic approach is that the client remains in control throughout the intervention. Furthermore, it is the client who identifies the need and hence the degree of commitment which this engenders is usually very high. Also, as a consequence of the trust that is generally built up during the intervention, it is more likely to get to the real problem.

In summary, although catalytic interventions sound complicated, they are often much simpler than they first appear. You will see from subsequent parts of this section that it is also an extremely versatile approach and, like acceptant, can be applied in many of the phases of a consulting assignment. Furthermore, once you have mastered how to intervene catalytically it can become a very comfortable style.

Underlying assumptions

As with acceptant interventions, the catalytic style is based on several important assumptions, including:

- The obvious assumption that the clients want to solve the problem and are capable of exploring various aspects of it with help.
- It is assumed that either additional data, or more structured data, will have a significant impact on client perception of the situation. Also, as a consequence of this change of perception, clients will be able to decide on an appropriate course of action.
- There is sufficient data within the client system to make a decision, although at present it may be difficult to access or interpret the data sensibly, or make a decision about change.
- There is likely to be greater commitment to a decision if it is owned by the clients. Hence, within a catalytic approach, it is essential that clients make their own decisions based on the data.

Again, as with the acceptant style, a catalytic approach can only be of value where these assumptions are satisfied. Where they are not, you will generally need to use other styles in combination with a catalytic approach.

How do I use a catalytic style?

Catalytic interventions seek to help clients collect or clarify data such that they can make their own decisions on what action to take. Enabling this to happen involves the following types of behaviour:

- Open body posture and eye contact similar to that used in the acceptant style;
- Attentive listening and confirmation of understanding;
- During catalytic interviews, using open questions to encourage clients to describe their situation—but also accepting the clients' perspective as the legitimate starting point to work on the problem or difficulty;
- Using focused listening and questioning skills to help clients explore their situation and illuminate some aspect of the subject—in particular using 'who', 'what', 'where', 'when' and 'how' questions;
- Using 'why' questions very carefully and infrequently in order to avoid creating an interrogatory atmosphere;
- Sometimes suggesting data-gathering methodologies in order to collect more information about a situation. These could include interview strategies, instruments or scales to measure performance, attitudes, perceptions or beliefs, survey methodology and action research. However, all suggestions must be made very tentatively—specific suggestions for action are not within the compass of the catalytic style;
- Giving support and encouragement as clients attempt to define or redefine the problem;
- Encouraging clients to make their own decisions—do not allow yourself to be drawn into making the decision for them. Equally, do not offer your opinion on which decision is best.

Over the years we have noted that during interviews many consultants who are new to this way of working experience real difficulty framing open catalytic questions. Very often their attempt at posing a catalytic question emerges more like a veiled prescription (e.g. Have you tried . . . ? You might find it useful to look at . . .). To help overcome this, we list below a few catalytic openings.

Statements and questions to help identify or explore the problem

- Tell me about the problem in your own words.
- What do you think caused that?
- Describe the situation now.
- How would you like things to be?
- What difficulties does that cause?
- What have you tried previously?
- What brought it to your attention?
- How do you see the situation developing?
- When did it first come to your notice?
- Who else is involved?
- Where else is it happening?

Questions to help define or redefine the problem

- Can you restate the problem in a phrase or sentence starting with the words 'how to . . .'? (this ensures ownership of the problem)
- How will you know if you have been successful?

Questions to help decision making

- What are the options?
- What are the advantages and disadvantages of each option?
- What would be the consequences?
- What would be your ideal solution?
- Which option will you choose?
- What are the implications in choosing that option?
- How will that option address the problem?

Questions to help implementation

- How will you implement the decision?
- Who else needs to be involved?
- What steps do you need to take?
- Where will you start?
- When will you do it?
- What resistance might you meet?
- How will you monitor progress?

What risks are involved?

Preliminary exercise

Before reading the rest of this section you might like to generate your own list of possible risks for both consultant and client when using a catalytic approach.

Perhaps the greatest risk for the consultant when using the catalytic style is inadvertently slipping into a style which is more like a veiled prescription. As a result we have named these veiled prescriptions 'prescriptive wolves in catalytic clothing'. They include a whole host of questions, which at first glance appear to be catalytic, but their real intention is to test out or suggest to the client a particular line of enquiry or way forward. A few examples include:

- Would it be a good idea if . . . ?
- Have you tried . . . ?
- Have you ever thought about trying . . . ?
- Why not try . . . ?
- What about . . . ?
- Why don't you . . . ?
- Do you think you could . . . ?
- How would you feel about trying . . . ?
- Would it be a good idea to try a . . ., b . . . or c . . . ?

In all these questions the client is being seduced along a path which the consultant has selected. In some cases it could be an appropriate path, but it is not within the remit of a catalytic approach.

A second but small risk for the consultant arises from the nature of catalytic interventions. As we have seen, the catalytic approach is restricted to addressing the client's felt needs. It is feasible, therefore, that as you only see the problem from the client's point of view you may lose your own perspective on the problem. In a sense the danger is that you can become as muddled and lost in your thinking as the client. Obviously, if this happens your value as a consultant is minimal.

From the client side, there are a number of other risks. These include:

- If you, as a consultant, lose your perspective it is highly likely that the clients will reject the whole approach. Similarly, it is feasible that clients could reject the idea that restructuring and/or gathering further data will contribute in any way towards resolving their problem.
- As the consultant works within the clients' felt needs it is possible that real needs will not be addressed, in which case you will end up resolving symptoms rather than the problem.
- Catalytic interventions usually lead to some form of decision and action by clients. However, as the responsibility for decision making remains with the clients, there is no guarantee that change will be in a positive direction. Hence it is important to help clients think through any consequences of change before they leap into action.
- Finally, if clients regularly call on a consultant for help it is possible that this will become a standard operating procedure. As a consequence, clients may discount any internal resources within their own organization as a source of help. We are aware of at least one company where the internal training department is discounted in favour of external help.

Having highlighted the risks, they do need to be kept in perspective. Other than the first, using veiled prescriptions, they are very small and in our view outweighed by the benefits of a catalytic style. In most cases clients welcome the approach. It is logical, diagnostic in nature and often matches their expectation of what a consultant should do; perhaps most important of all, the clients remain firmly in charge throughout.

When can I use a catalytic style? Catalytic interventions are extremely versatile and, as with acceptant, may be used at most points during an assignment. For example, during initial contact and gaining entry catalytic interventions may be used to find out more about the clients and their department. In contracting they can be used to explore, clarify and check out contractual details. From the earlier discussion it will be obvious that in data gathering catalytic interventions are essential. Indeed, all the data-gathering techniques and presentation methods discussed in Chapters 6 and 7 can be used to support a catalytic approach.

In decision making the catalytic style can help clients think through the consequences of any decision, and during implementation to check progress. During disengagement it can be used to explore any possibility for further work.

Where clients are thinking in terms of an ideal solution, they may need help to recognize they have a problem and not a puzzle. Furthermore, they could need help to clarify that a 100 per cent solution might not exist and perhaps the best that can be attained is 60 per cent. In this situation a catalytic approach can be useful to help them check out options and outcomes. A simple example is how to get the best possible job done within a restricted budget.

Catalytic interventions can also be of value where the clients do not have the confidence to make a decision; for example, where the action is likely to be unpalatable. As a catalytic consultant you can help clients explore the options available in order to build their confidence in the decision. In this sense the catalytic style can be developmental; it helps clients to make their own decisions in the future.

Catalytic style in practice

To conclude this section we include two examples of the catalytic approach in action. The first illustrates how it can help build commitment towards a decision which has already been taken. The organization concerned had already decided at a senior level to introduce a formal procedure for staff development. However, managers at the next level down, who would be responsible for implementing the procedure, were suspicious of the change. Our role involved working with the management group to help them develop skills to carry out staff development. Unfortunately, one particular group spent a great deal of time dwelling on the disadvantages of the new system. To overcome this we simply invited them to discuss and list the advantages and disadvantages to staff development. The result was that they began to recognize that the positive aspects of staff development outweighed their reservations. By the end of our intervention they had become much more committed and enthusiastic about implementing the change.

Clearly, choosing a catalytic intervention was risky—the group might have reinforced their negative perceptions of staff development. However, we believed that allowing them to arrive at their own conclusion would engender more commitment than if we had tried either 'selling' the new system or telling them they had no choice about complying. In the event the risk proved to be worth taking.

The second illustration involved a team development assignment with a group of eight senior managers. Quite early in the work it became apparent that each of them was working to a different agenda. To make progress we invited them to write down individually what they saw as the main purpose for the group's existence. As we expected (but to their surprise) we received eight very different responses and the group had to engage in a considerable amount of further work to agree their purpose. Eventually this led to much improved teamwork. Before our intervention they had assumed they were all working towards a common purpose, and they needed this kind of catalytic intervention to demonstrate that individually they were all going in different directions.

To conclude, the catalytic style would be useful in:

- Helping managers and their staff explore their expectations of each other so that they have a better idea of their needs, rather than relying merely on job descriptions.
- Conducting a survey to help managers discover which aspects of their management style are considered by their staff to be unhelpful.
- Conducting a survey to find out how members of a team view their current performance; helping them generate ideas on how they would like to work and then helping them make decisions about how to achieve it.
- Helping managers and their subordinates to compare and contrast their perceptions and judgements about the subordinates' performance (as an alternative to the merely prescriptive appraisal).
- Helping individuals and groups surface their assumptions and stereotypes about each other which are causing them to take a negative, uncooperative approach to each other: Sales v. Marketing, Service v. Sales, Planning v. Operations, Branch v. Head Office, Management v. Trade Unions or Men v. Women.
- Helping groups to improve their creativity by teaching them techniques such as lateral thinking and brainstorming.

Overall, catalytic interventions are designed to help clients make sense of the data they already have or to enable them to assess what extra data they need to make a valid diagnosis of the problem.

They also allow clients to increase their knowledge, understanding and awareness of the situation, and develop and distribute information around the system, thereby accelerating the rate of change to a new way of operating.

Summary
- Catalytic interventions involve helping the client address felt needs by clarifying existing data and/or gathering additional data. They can utilize a variety of data-gathering, analysis and presentation methods.
- Relevant data could include objective facts and numbers but also more exotic data such as feelings and behaviour.
- The responsibility for decision making remains with the client.
- Catalytic interventions assume that:
  - data absence or overload is causing the difficulty
  - relevant data exists within the client system
  - clarifying/gathering data will enable the client to progress
- Catalytic interventions employ behaviour which:
  - accepts and acknowledges the client's felt needs
  - uses focused open questions and/or data clarification/gathering methodologies
  - presents the client's data in a meaningful way
  - gives the client support and encouragement
- Catalytic interventions involve several risks, but the greatest is that the consultant will slip into using veiled prescriptions.

Confrontational interventional style

One common form of confrontation involves situations where the clients are part of the problem and there are discrepancies between what they say they do (or think) and what they actually do (or think) in practice. Confrontation highlights the mismatch between thoughts, beliefs or values and behaviour. However, at the outset of an assignment clients will not usually be aware of any discrepancy. We are full of contradictions and mismatches between what we believe and what we do. For example, at a personal level we may believe that 'healthy living' is important for everyone, yet in practice we probably take little (if any) exercise, follow a convenience food diet, and drink more than we should. Or we may say it is important to value and respect others, yet in practice our listening skills leave much to be desired. We would suggest that for most of us (the authors included) these kinds of discrepancies are commonplace.

The same phenomena occur in client systems within organizations. For example, managers may believe that customer satisfaction is important yet in practice they continually overlook late deliveries, shoddy goods and poor service. Very often, rather than addressing the discrepancy, they make excuses to rationalize the mistakes and then continue in the same self-defeating way. An illustration of this happened recently to one of the authors. He took a punctured tyre to a local garage for repair. The tyre was left late on a Saturday afternoon to be picked up on the following Monday afternoon. As it happened he could not retrieve the tyre on Monday but called in on Tuesday instead. Despite the fact that the garage advertised 'Customer Satisfaction is our Priority', the tyre was not ready. He was offered the explanation that the garage had too much work on. Rather than confront the discrepancy with the sales assistant (who was probably only a tiny cog in the client system) the author took the tyre elsewhere. This time he chose a garage that did not advertise 'customer satisfaction' but had the job done immediately.

This theme has its parallel with most people in most organizations, although we do not believe that such discrepancies happen deliberately or as a result of malice. It is more that as individuals or organizations we are either not aware of the differences or choose not to acknowledge them. It is only when a discrepancy is pointed out that we might try to change. This 'pointing out' is the substance of confrontation.

The difficulty lies in confusion between confrontation and conflict. As will be discussed later, there is a danger that confrontation may generate conflict, although, when carried out effectively, confrontation simply highlights discrepancies. It is not about scoring points, making value judgements, getting 'one-up' on the clients, or teaching them a lesson. Confrontation in consulting terms is objective and non-judgemental. Conflict, on the other hand, is often handled by trying to win and this can generate antagonism and hostility.

Confronting a client may also generate an emotional response. You might have noticed an emotional reaction within yourself as you read the first paragraph of this section where we mentioned two common discrepancies at a personal level. This gives some indication of the difficulty in using confrontation. Part of the problem is that there is no way of predicting how the client will respond. Even quite gentle confrontation may be heard as serious criticism and the emotional response can be completely out of proportion to the discrepancy being highlighted. We have found that even positive confrontation can evoke an unexpected emotional response. We can illustrate this with an example drawn from one of our training programmes on consulting skills. During the programme we always attempt to tackle confrontation experientially, often by confronting the group ourselves and encouraging other participants to confront issues which they feel are significant. The substance of any confrontation is always based on discrepancies as they arise during the programme. This could involve a range of issues such as participation within the group, participants psychologically opting out, talking over the top of one another, or poor listening. During the early stages of one particular programme much of this type of behaviour was evident within the group. However, as time went by they started to change and by the time we reached confrontation their behaviour was consistent with the contract we had agreed at the start of the programme. They were listening to one another, valuing one another's contributions, participating openly and honestly, etc. We decided, therefore, to confront the group by reviewing the initial contract and then describing in concrete terms how they had developed and changed as the programme went along. Our intention was to reinforce the very positive changes that had taken place and encourage them to continue with the behaviour which was now evident. This was eventually the outcome, but the immediate emotional reaction of the group was astonishing. They became defensive, attempted to deny our observations and generally tried to discount the intervention. We were surprised because from our point of view the confrontation was very positive. Needless to say, it was a salutary lesson.

This example also illustrates that confronting clients does not involve blame or judgement; it simply acknowledges what was agreed (in this case, the contract) and points out how the clients have behaved subsequently. That is, it highlights what the clients said they would do and what they have actually done. However, the choice of what to do about the discrepancy remains firmly with the clients. Confronting does not involve telling them what you think is best, or what you would do under similar circumstances.

So far we have concentrated on a method of confronting that highlights discrepancies between what the clients think and what they do. However, there are two other ways of confronting which are equally valid. The first involves highlighting the implications of continuing with a current behaviour pattern. For example, you might like to think about your behaviour when you cross a road. If your habit involves looking left, right, then left again, ponder the implications of this if you try to cross roads in France. The other method of confronting clients involves pointing out the impact they are having on you. We recall one particular manager who, when under pressure, unconsciously raised his voice level to a point where he was nearly shouting. Our confrontation involved highlighting his behaviour and then describing how we felt on the receiving end of his tirade. From discussion later we discovered that this was the first time he had ever received this kind of feedback, and from then on he consciously attempted to change the habit.

We have already mentioned that confrontation is practically always accompanied by some form of emotional reaction. Regardless of which method of confronting you choose, clients will *feel* confronted and may react in an emotional way. A further mild example of confrontation involves calling attention to some particular client behaviour which you find unacceptable, pointing out that you don't understand it and asking for an explanation. This has important implications for how you act. First, your initial confrontation statement will need to be very clear. If you are confronting about something that the client is failing to do, it may well be heard as criticism. Under these conditions it is quite possible that your statement will be misinterpreted. Hence, the clearer it is at the start the better. Linked to this, it is essential that your confrontation is based on solid data which you have either observed or experienced. It is folly to embark on a confrontation which is based on second-hand or controversial data. Likewise, data which is historical is not very useful. Such data is likely to be denied by the client and your attempt at confrontation will fail.

Having confronted the client you will probably need to switch to an acceptant style to acknowledge and deal with the feelings which have been stirred up. However, this does not mean denying the substance of the confrontation—switching to an acceptant style is simply the most appropriate way of dealing with the feelings.

By now you will probably have recognized that confrontation can be a high-risk intervention style. As such it needs a solid base of trust between you and the client. In particular the client needs to feel valued and supported throughout the intervention. Without this the probability of success will be very low. Also it is worth noting that confronting large client systems such as groups can take a long time to work through. Inevitably, where many individuals are involved the feelings generated are varied and complex. As a result group confrontation is much more complicated than with an individual client. Indeed, given the level of risk involved, it is always worth assessing your own feelings and motives before starting to confront. Your intervention must genuinely attempt to help the client rather than satisfy any personal need for self-gratification. Also, if you feel particularly uncomfortable using the style your own feelings can interfere and reduce the impact of the intervention.

Nevertheless, despite all the difficulties and risks, confrontation is a very important consulting style and at times is essential. It is a very powerful way of working and can prompt clients into action more rapidly than any of the previous styles. As such it cannot be overlooked or ignored simply because it is risky.

Underlying assumptions

As with the two styles discussed earlier, confrontation is based on a few important assumptions:

- The clients' values, beliefs and behaviour are a part of the problem that you are trying to resolve.
- Currently, the clients do not have insight into (or choose to ignore) discrepancies between their espoused values and their behaviour and/or the impact and implications of their current behaviour.
- If the discrepancies or implications of behaviour are addressed the clients will have sufficient resources of their own to find a solution or satisfactory way forward with the problem.
- The clients have sufficient emotional resilience to undertake an examination of their behaviour and values and will be able to deal with the feelings likely to be engendered as a result.

Obviously, for a confrontation to be effective, all these assumptions must be satisfied. However, as we have seen, the method is unlikely to be used in isolation. More typically, confrontation forms only a small part of your work with clients and is generally used in conjunction with other styles.

How do I use a confrontational style?

Confronting clients usually involves one or more of three actions:

- Pointing out discrepancies between what they think they do and what they actually do;
- Pointing out the implications of continuing with current behaviour;
- Confronting clients with your own feelings about their behaviour.

To carry out these actions effectively requires the following behavioural skills:

- Adopting an open body posture, eye contact and attentive listening;
- Using direct questions that help clients towards awareness and honesty;
- Presenting facts, counter-arguments and logic to help clients test their objectivity;
- Confronting the clients with discrepancies between their perception and their behaviour and/or their beliefs or values and their behaviour;
- Pointing out to clients the impact of their behaviour on you. This is sometimes known as immediacy or 'you-me talk';
- Helping clients examine any implications which could arise as a consequence of their behaviour;
- Presenting alternative frames of reference for clients to consider;
- Towards the end of the confrontation, summarizing any decision which has been taken.

What risks are involved?

Preliminary exercise
Before reading the rest of this section you might like to generate your own list of possible risks for both consultant and client when using a confrontational approach.

We have already acknowledged confrontation as a risky method of working, but to keep this in perspective we need to examine more fully the risks involved. For the consultant the greatest risk is allowing the confrontation to degenerate into argument. Usually this happens if we move away from objective statements about what we have observed or experienced and start making value judgements about what the client should be doing. In consulting terms this is fatal. Obviously, as human beings we cannot avoid making judgements, but these should not interfere with our behaviour when attempting to confront a client.

Beyond this, there are a number of other risks which need to be kept in mind:

- If the confrontation is inappropriate or badly timed you could be rejected by the clients and the assignment terminated.
- Once you have started the confrontation and made your opening statement, control of the situation passes to the clients. Also, there is no way of predicting how the clients will react.
- In some cases clients could refuse to accept responsibility for the problem or their own behaviour and instead attempt to blame you— the 'it's your fault' scenario.
- It is feasible that at the end of the confrontation your relationship with the clients will have deteriorated.
- Even if your confrontation of the clients is well done it is likely that you will get denial, justification, argument, counter-argument, displacement, projection and blame. It is important that you prepare yourself, accept it and do not get into win/lose arguments.
- It is also worth remembering that, if you unexpectedly find yourself on the receiving end of such behaviour from your clients, you may well have been operating confrontationally even if you did not intend to do so.

When confronting groups there are at least two additional risks:

- Confronting a group invariably takes time, and sometimes a long time. As we mentioned earlier, the emotional reactions with a group are varied and unpredictable and take time to work through. It is therefore very risky to start confronting a group if you are faced with severe time restrictions. The results are likely to be incomplete, leading to dissatisfaction all round.
- When groups face confrontation they are highly likely to feel threatened. As a consequence they may 'gang up' on the consultant in an attempt to undermine, deny or ridicule the substance of the confrontation and as a result merely consolidate their current behaviour.

Needless to say, confronting a group should be undertaken with extreme care. However, for the clients there are a few other risks:

- First, the clients may feel hurt, perhaps even betrayed. From their perspective you were invited in to help and yet it appears that all you have to offer feels like personal criticism.
- Linked to personal hurt, there is a danger that the clients' self-image could be undermined. We all have a picture of ourselves and how we interact with the world. Destructive confrontation could challenge this picture, leaving clients feeling worthless.

- Within confrontation clients remain responsible for decision making, but there is no guarantee that their decision will improve the situation. It is possible that the problem could become even worse as a result of the intervention.
- Finally, poorly judged confrontation could prove too difficult or too much for the clients to take in. As a consequence they may simply deny the whole intervention.

Given all these risks associated with confrontation, you may be left feeling that it is not worth trying and the costs of failure are too high. Nevertheless, despite the risks, there are times when confrontation becomes essential. There is no point continuing with an assignment when it is clear that it will fail; confrontation may be the only option to promote reassessment and change. If you should confront your clients and you don't, they are probably entitled to question whether you are as effective as you should be.

When can I use a confrontational style?

Confrontation is different in both nature and application to the two styles discussed earlier. Unlike the others it is not a style which is likely to be used over a long period of time. Indeed, in some cases the actual confrontation may consist of a single sentence. However, the level of feeling generated as a result could require you to switch to an acceptant style to deal with the feelings. Also, as we have seen, in order for confrontation to be effective there needs to be a high level of trust between you and the clients and this takes time to build up. It follows therefore that confrontation is rarely used during the early phases of consulting (i.e. during initial contact and gaining entry). Obviously, this cannot be a hard and fast rule and there are exceptions; for example, where part of a client system is being extremely defensive and will not allow you to gain entry. The only way forward might be to confront them with the implications of their behaviour, although this is risky. If you have not gained entry you have no way of judging whether the level of trust is appropriate. But it could be a case where you have no other option—in a sense you are damned if you do and damned if you don't!

More usually, confrontation is needed later in an assignment. During contracting it may be of value as a tool to help clients ensure that all the important items have been covered. Similarly, later on, it could be used to instigate re-examination of the contract where clients are failing to complete their side of the agreement. During data gathering it could be used to highlight discrepancies or omissions in the data; in decision making it can help clients face up to uncomfortable decisions or decisions where they need to recognize that they are part of the problem. Finally, confrontation can also have a place during disengagement, particularly where the clients attempt to procrastinate over the end of the assignment (perhaps wishing to cling on for additional reassurance).

Despite the risks, confrontation is a valuable consulting tool. Exactly how it can be used will become clear from the illustrations that follow.

Confrontational interventions in use

Our first example of confrontation is interesting in that it illustrates a situation where the problem under discussion was also present in the 'here and now' of the immediate client group. The actual assignment involved helping the client organization to introduce total quality management. At the time of the confrontation we were working intensively with the senior management team to develop a strategy to introduce the change. The particular issue they were discussing was how to get the staff to participate in the new approach. Our confrontation involved highlighting the fact that the same issue was present within the group. They were discussing how to get others to participate but had not recognized that several people had been ignored during the discussion and had stopped participating. Having made the intervention the group immediately reacted defensively, suggesting all the reasons why participation was difficult, claiming we did not understand their particular situation, etc. In response we switched to an acceptant approach to acknowledge and deal with their feelings, but at the same time held firmly to the content of our confrontation.

Eventually, as the feelings began to subside, the group began to recognize that in order for total quality management to succeed fundamental changes had to take place in both staff behaviour and their own management style. One could not happen without the other. Furthermore, it would be highly unlikely that the staff could be encouraged to change unless there was a visible change in the way they were managed.

A second illustration of confrontation involved a colleague of ours who was invited to work with an organization to examine whether managerial behaviour took adequate account of equal opportunity legislation. In retrospect we are convinced that the senior management group believed their organization to be free from any problems (in effect the consultant's engagement was to 'rubber stamp' what they believed was obvious). Unfortunately, the more the consultant probed the more she discovered this was not the case. She found that many managers were regularly acting in a discriminatory manner and it was merely good fortune which had protected them from legal action. Once the data had been collected the consultant confronted the senior group with her evidence. This caused uproar; they attempted to deny the data, discredit the consultant and undermine the data-collection method, all in an attempt to maintain the *status quo*. Fortunately, the consultant was experienced in this kind of work and had anticipated an emotional response. She was able to switch to a more acceptant style to deal with the group's reaction.

Eventually the feelings subsided and the group was able to address the information more rationally and plan appropriate changes. In conversation later it was evident that the consultant knew that there was no easy option for this assignment. Challenging the senior group's belief about their organization was bound to be stormy, but to have colluded with their view would have been a recipe for professional disaster.

A third, more common illustration of confrontation can be found in many training situations. Most trainers who have used video as a means of giving feedback will have encountered individual or group resistance at some point. It is worth pondering why. There is no doubt that, when used sensitively, video can be a very powerful feedback mechanism. However, when on the receiving end, video confronts individuals with an action replay of how they behave in any given situation. Even without comments from the trainer this can be highly confrontational. If a consultant's verbal comments can evoke a powerful reaction from clients it is hardly surprising that the prospect of video on a training course can be equally frightening. Obviously, video has its place in training but it should be used by trainers who can easily adopt an acceptant style to deal with the feelings it generates.

A final illustration of confrontation occurred with another colleague of ours who was employed as a technical training officer within a large organization. When the problem came to light his department had just completed a long series of courses designed to help the workforce develop their reinstatement skills (i.e. filling in and resurfacing holes which have been dug in public highways to gain access to essential service pipes). The problem started when our colleague was called in by a director to be told that reinstatement was not being done properly. Despite the training that had already been carried out, in the director's view the workforce did not know what they were doing and would require immediate retraining. Our colleague was dumbfounded; he could not believe what he was being told. Rather than accept the problem at face value he decided to find out more. As a first step he invited into the training centre a sample of the workforce and asked them to carry out a reinstatement exercise. The results demonstrated they knew exactly what to do, and hence the problem was not one of deficiency in skill or knowledge.

Armed with these results he went back to confront the director. Effectively, the confrontation consisted of agreeing with the director that reinstatement was ineffective but also of showing that when tested in the training centre the workforce knew perfectly well what to do. The problem therefore was not one of lack of training. Eventually, the director begrudgingly accepted that the only way to discover the root of the problem was for the training officer to investigate further. The resulting on-the-job interviews and investigation revealed that the problem lay in insufficient availability of tools and equipment, poor scheduling for delivery of reinstatement materials and inadequate supervision. Without the confrontation the organization would have spent a fortune on unnecessary retraining, the reputation of the training department would have been seriously undermined, and the real causes would not have come to light. As it turned out, the correct problem was tackled and the reputation of training enhanced.

In conclusion, confrontational style would be useful in:

- Helping a member or members of a group challenge what they see as inappropriate norms of behaviour which the rest of the group accept without question.
- Helping an individual or a group challenge the difference between

what managers say they will do and what they do in practice so that both parties are able to deal with the possible bad feelings.

- Helping two or more groups to deal with the consequences of a clash between their differing norms and standards, which can often produce rationalization, justification and projection.
- Helping two or more groups deal with the stereotyping that often leads to discriminatory behaviour, e.g. men and women, blacks and whites, or able-bodied people and the disabled.
- Helping a whole organization by challenging assumptions that hinder effectiveness and change and prevent the move towards becoming a quality organization.

Overall, confrontational interventions help people to see the discontinuity between their stated intentions or beliefs and their actual behaviour or the implications of continuing their current behaviour pattern.

Summary

- Confronting involves:
  - pointing out discrepancies between espoused action and action in practice;
  - pointing out the implications of behaviour;
  - pointing out the impact of behaviour.
- Confrontation inevitably involves feelings which cannot be predicted.
- Confrontation does not involve blame or judgement, neither does it tell clients what to do. All decision making as a result remains the responsibility of the clients.
- Effective confrontation requires a firm base of trust with clients.
- Confronting a group is inevitably more complex and takes longer.
- Confrontation assumes that:
  - clients are part of the problem;
  - currently the clients do not have insight into the issue to be confronted;
  - once confronted, clients will have sufficient resources to find their own solution.
- Confrontation is a high-risk intervention style, the greatest risk being that the intervention will generate conflict. Confronting a group needs particular care.
- Confrontation is generally used more in the middle and later stages of an assignment, i.e. from contracting onwards.

Prescriptive intervention style

Although prescription is probably the most commonly used intervention style it is often used inappropriately. As mentioned earlier, it is the traditional style used in medical consultations between doctor and patient, where the doctor diagnoses the patient's problem and prescribes an appropriate remedy. As a way of helping it is rooted in the concept of the 'expert'—that is, someone who is accredited in, and can call upon, a body of expert knowledge or skill to find solutions for particular client problems. Although traditionally a medical or legal intervention style, it has over the years been adopted by many other specialists, e.g. health and safety, personnel, information technology, legal and financial.

When appropriate, there is no doubt that a prescriptive approach can be of real value. The main advantage is that it is expedient and usually leads to results more quickly than any other consulting style. Unfortunately, this can be deceptively appealing to clients. Most consultants will report a great deal of client pressure for them to generate solutions to problems. Indeed, why not? If solutions lead to rapid results then what is the point of wasting time using other intervention styles? In this respect a solution may offer clients a very seductive 'quick fix'. Take, for example, the personal illustration of losing weight. The solution in this case may be for the overweight client to follow a diet. Dieticians, health educationalists and medical experts can offer a host of different diets, or the overweight client can buy a book on dieting (and there are hundreds, if not thousands, to choose from).

The difficulty is that diets alone rarely work in the long term. The majority of people who diet lose weight initially but within a few months return to their original weight (and probably bemoan their problem and look round for a new diet). The difficulty with weight loss is that it is about changing eating habits (i.e. changing lifestyle) and this is not easy. More effective weight-loss programmes tend to be those which support people while they make lifestyle adjustments. But unfortunately the 'quick fix' diet solution is still very seductive despite the fact that it rarely works. Hence the enormous sales figures for diet books.

In organizations the seductive influence of solution-oriented consulting is the same. Take, of example, early approaches to the management of quality of goods or services. The key at that time appeared to be simply introducing quality control (QC) but, in retrospect, we can see that quality control alone only took the problem away from both management and staff and placed it squarely with the quality control department. The job of QC was conceived as one of overseeing and advising on the quality of the product (or service). Unfortunately, 'overseeing and advising' quickly became perceived more as a policing role. The problem of quality became synonymous with the QC department. By contrast, total quality management (TQM) attempts to harness the whole organization in a coordinated effort towards continuous improvement in quality. This is a totally different concept to quality control and requires fundamental changes in how organizations function. Although TQM does not offer a prescriptive 'quick fix' it is perhaps a better route for tackling quality problems.

Within the prescriptive style consultants (explicitly or implicitly) perceive themselves as experts in their field, able to diagnose the clients' real problem and advise on an appropriate course of action. The main aim of the advice is to give guidance to clients who otherwise would not know what to do. When used under these circumstances prescription can prove to be a highly effective consulting style. However, on the deficit side, prescriptive interventions do not allow the clients any opportunity for development or growth. Admittedly, given an appropriate intervention, the problem will be solved, but the clients gain no insight into how the solution was generated. Knowledge of how consultants arrive at a solution is part of their specialist expertise (and is not a subject to be shared with clients). As a result, the clients will need to call on the consultant again if the problem ever recurs.

Blake and Mouton (1976, 1983) highlight a further difficulty with prescription. When working with client systems that comprise groups or organizations, they argue:

> answers usually are directed to the top of the system so that the system's power/authority–obedience structure can be used to mandate the changes. Under these circumstances, implementation is more likely to occur, but resistance will almost certainly be generated at lower levels. Perceived coercion will eventually cause the prescribed changes to become distorted, watered down or simply ignored.

Finally, it is important to acknowledge the seductive attraction of prescription as a consulting style. There is no doubt that it can be a very powerful style and offer to the consultant a great deal of personal gratification. Clients may even wish to be hidden safely under the wing of an expert who can provide wise and thoughtful answers. Helping clients and at the same time being recognized as the purveyor of help can have immense appeal. But, as we have begun to indicate, it does have severe limitations.

Nevertheless, despite the limitations, there are times when prescription can be the most appropriate consulting style to use. In order to recognize these occasions we turn next to the assumptions behind the mode.

Underlying assumptions

The assumptions which underlie prescriptive interventions are a little different to those found in the other styles. First, there is a set of three basic assumptions, which lie behind all prescriptions. Then, coupled to the basic assumptions, there are three more which relate to particular conditions.

Basic assumptions

- The consultant is an expert in a specialism appropriate to the client's problem and is able to give sound advice.
- The consultant will be able to provide a satisfactory solution to the problem.
- The client will comply with and carry out the prescription.

Conditional assumptions

- The client is genuinely floundering and does not know what to do, or does not possess the relevant skills to find a satisfactory solution to the problem.

or

- The situation is critical and requires expedient action. Under such circumstances it is usually obvious to all concerned that unilateral decisions, direction and speed of action are of paramount importance.

or

- The client simply wants the problem alleviated and is happy to hand over all control and responsibility to the consultant.

How do I use a prescriptive style?

Prescriptive interventions attempt to move the client towards accepting a consultant-generated solution. This could involve the following patterns of behaviour:

- Using a strictly professional approach, often paying little regard to social or personal pleasantries.
- Conducting a probing diagnostic investigation to determine what you need to know about the situation.
- Listening to clients but with a view to diagnosing the problem and offering a solution.
- Taking control of the intervention by telling clients directly how you perceive the problem or situation.
- Giving expert advice—prescribing the 'best' solution or set of actions for the clients to follow.
- Describing your solution with confidence and authority and if necessary offering to supervise implementation.
- In instances where clients are unwilling to adopt the solution, you may threaten to terminate the assignment and, if necessary, actually do so. However, it is important to leave the door open by suggesting to clients that when they require help they can get in touch.

It is also important to emphasize two further points:

- Few consultants follow prescription in this pure form. More often prescriptions and advice are offered as suggestions or recommendations in the hope that these will be more palatable to the clients. Nevertheless, the underlying theme of the intervention is the same. All that has changed is the flavour of the medicine.
- A prescriptive approach can describe what to do in the sense of outlining a set of actions to solve a technical problem, but it can also prescribe behavioural change. Of the two, the technical forms of prescription tend to be much the easier for clients to accept and apply.

What risks are involved?

Preliminary exercise
Before reading the rest of this section you might like to generate your own list of possible risks for both consultant and client when using a prescriptive approach.

Perhaps the greatest risk in using a prescriptive approach is that it creates dependency within the relationship. Although the problem may be alleviated through the consultant's solution, the clients gain little insight into how the solution was derived. Hence, if a similar problem arises in the future clients must return to the consultant for further help. You might argue this is a good way of ensuring further business, but in our view this kind of approach (when used excessively) does not foster healthy client–consultant relationships. The more that clients become dependent on a consultant, the more they are likely to begin to resent the inequality of the relationship.

Aside from this there are a few other risks which should be taken into account:

- Prescriptions rarely include alternatives. The nature of a prescription is such that it informs clients what to do. If clients find the solution unacceptable for some reason they have no option other than to reject the prescription altogether.
- The clients may not be sufficiently competent to implement the prescription.
- In situations where the prescription is cascaded down through a client system, subsequent levels who become involved may modify, water down, or ignore the prescribed changes.
- For the consultant, there is a risk of being rejected if the clients perceive the solution to be unacceptable.
- Also, as consultants accept total responsibility for diagnosing the problem and generating a solution, their professional competence is under the spotlight. Any mistake or error of judgement could easily lead to accusations of professional incompetence or neglect, in some cases perhaps leading to lengthy and expensive litigation.
- In order to generate an appropriate solution the problem must lie within the consultant's field of expertise. In organizations this may not be the case—many organizational problems are multi-functional. As a consequence, the consultant could end up treating symptoms rather than problems.

Take, for example, the problem of high sickness absence. The real problem could lie in any one or more of several specialist areas, such as:

- occupational health — through a genuinely unhealthy workplace
- ergonomics — through poorly designed working areas
- personnel — through poor reward and appraisal systems
- management — through excessively authoritarian management behaviour

It is difficult to envisage any one expert who is likely to be able to span such a wide variety of differing specialist areas, so a single specialist solution might not adequately solve the problem.

When can I use a prescriptive style?

Three important uses of prescription follow automatically from the conditional assumptions discussed earlier:

- First, prescription is appropriate when the clients are floundering and genuinely do not know what to do or do not possess suitable skills. However, it is sometimes difficult to determine whether clients are genuinely floundering or have some other reason for not tackling the problem. Fortunately, there is one clue that may be available. If you find when describing your solution to clients that they respond with 'Yes, but . . . ' (that is, finding reasons why your prescription will not work), then it is a fair bet they are not actually floundering and some other intervention style would be more appropriate.
- A second use for prescription is in situations which are critical or where there is a severe time constraint which demands expedient

action. All other consulting styles take time and sometimes a long time. By contrast, prescription is fast and leads to quick results.

- The third use of prescriptions is where clients simply want a solution and are not interested in anything beyond that.

Within the phases of consultation, prescription is likely to be used after data gathering and decision making. However, in this case, it is the consultant who makes all the decisions on behalf of the client. Only the outcome and advice on appropriate action are fed back to the client towards the end of the assignment.

Prescriptive style in practice

You will have gathered by now that prescription is a style which is appropriate much less frequently than any of the others. We suspect that the number of occasions you will be called on to deal with critical situations will be very few, hence the only situations where prescription is likely to be appropriate are where the client is floundering or needs a solution quickly. In our experience such conditions are not very common and as a consequence our illustrations of prescriptive interventions are quite limited.

Our first example of prescription happened to one of the authors when he was working as personal counsellor within a large industrial organization. At that time many of his clients were individuals who, for one reason or another, were coming to terms with a variety of life crises. As such they were often depressed or suffering from anxiety. However, one particular client was of an order of magnitude different from the rest. At the time of the first interview he clearly exhibited extreme anxiety symptoms—obvious trembling, emotionally very upset, unable to concentrate, and at times unable to string a logical sentence together. Although the author was used to helping clients suffering with anxiety, this was altogether different. It quickly became evident that some action had to be taken immediately to help control the client's symptoms. The author advised the client to seek immediate medical help from his GP and offered to make an appointment on the client's behalf. The client gratefully accepted the offer and the GP made arrangements for an urgent interview. When the client returned a few days later, having received a prescription for medication from the GP, he was in a much more stable condition and more traditional counselling took place. Although the author did not like using a prescriptive style to tell the client he needed to see his doctor, in retrospect it was probably the most helpful course of action.

A second simple illustration of prescription involved a personnel officer who was approached by a manager for help with a job advertisement. The manager was attempting to fill a vacancy in his department and had drafted an advertisement for the local press. Unfortunately, the way the advertisement had been written was clearly discriminatory and could have led to problems later. As time was short the personnel officer prescriptively pointed out the discriminatory sections and offered to redraft the advertisement, taking account of current employment legislation. The manager accepted the prescription, recognizing there were aspects of personnel work which were outside his field of expertise and best left to an expert.

In conclusion, the prescriptive style would be useful on these occasions:

- Helping clients out of a crisis situation where they might be unable or unwilling to take action, e.g. an emergency such as a fire or the need to abandon ship.
- Helping clients out of crisis situations where they are incapable of making their own decisions because of loss of confidence, are immobilized or unable to cope.
- When you, as the consultant, have the right answer to a problem and withholding the information will lead to the problem not being solved.
- When you have not been able to help clients generate their own solutions and confronting the issue has not worked, then it may be appropriate to be prescriptive.
- Preventing clients from taking precipitate action which may prejudice alternative courses of action that could be generated with mature or more objective thought.
- To help poorly functioning clients take decisive steps to get out of the situation which is causing the distress, thereby stopping the restrictive and self-destructive behaviour.

Overall, prescriptive interventions are used to help people who are in no position to make their own decisions and therefore need someone to diagnose their problem and tell them what to do to solve it. The basic premise is that the consultant is an expert and the client is prepared to accept the answers the consultant provides.

Summary
- Prescription is probably the most commonly used consulting style.
- Prescriptive interventions are expedient and probably lead to results more quickly than any other consulting style. As a consequence, prescriptive 'quick fix' solutions can be very seductive.
- Within prescription consultants perceive themselves as experts able to diagnose the client's real problem and prescribe an appropriate course of action.
- Prescriptive interventions assume that:
  - the consultant is an expert and can provide expert solutions
  - the client will accept the solution
  - the client is genuinely floundering; or the situation is critical; or the client simply needs the problem solved
- Prescriptive interventions require the consultant to:
  - conduct a probing diagnostic investigation
  - give a complete description of the problem to the client
  - give expert advice on the best solution or next set of actions
  - if necessary, offer to supervise implementation of the prescription
- Prescriptive interventions involve several risks:
  - generating client dependency
  - client rejection of the prescription or the consultant

- where the prescription is cascaded down, modification, dilution or ignoring the prescription
- in the case of error, accusations of professional incompetence
- consultants not recognizing when they step outside their field of expertise

3 Consulting skills

Skills for a client-centred consultant

Most consultants spend years developing the technical skills required to do their jobs. Yet often very little attention is paid to the skills they require to become successful change agents. Perhaps the reason for this is that these are exactly the same skills we require for everyday social intercourse. We tend to take them for granted, assuming that they are common sense. Unfortunately, the one certain thing we can say about common sense is that it isn't very common.

Talking of the skills that underlie effective consulting reminds me of the professional golfer who demonstrated his skill by doing trick shots. He could pile three balls on top of each other and hit the middle one; hit the ball so that it swung round and came back to him; then twist it in a circle. He could do anything with the ball, he would say, but make it talk. Yet when asked if he could hit six balls out of six straight down the middle of the fairway, he would always say that he couldn't guarantee that. What seems simple is often the most difficult to do. The same is true of consulting.

Client-centred consulting involves managing relationships with your clients and often involves you in helping them to manage relationships with each other. If you are to do this effectively you need to follow the phases of the consulting cycle and you need facility in a range of consulting styles. All this requires a range of basic skills. We have grouped these skills into seven separate categories:

Knowing yourself   Successful client-centred consultants are aware of their strengths and weaknesses and how they impact on others, and have a strategy for their self-development.

Communication skills   If you are a consultant you are a professional communicator. You must be able to express your ideas and be able to understand others at all levels of your organization.

Observation and feedback skills   Whenever you are working with a client group, whatever the issue, you need to be aware of how relationships and behaviour in the group are affecting the problem. You need a high level of observation skills to enable you to be aware of what is happening in the group and to feed it back to the client.

Problem-solving skills   You are likely to have knowledge of a number of problem-solving techniques as part of your technical expertise. However, the more client-centred you are the more you will need to involve your clients and client groups in the problem-solving and decision-making process. You need skills in helping groups to look at problems together, generate creative ideas, examine the options and finally make decisions that they are all committed to.

Team building   Organizational change always has an impact on the way people work together in teams. Often part of your role as a consultant is to assist your client group to be a strong and effective team. This means you will be involved in helping team members to listen to each other and value each other; take a flexible approach to problem solving; deal with uncomfortable and risky interpersonal issues; confront issues to do with leadership style; and deal with each other's feelings.

Dealing with people's feelings   It may be stating the glaringly obvious to say that change agents are in the business of change. But it is our experience that consultants often try to drive through changes in technology or procedures or structure without recognizing the impact these changes will have on people in the organization. Those who are in the throes of change inevitably experience feelings, even when they themselves have chosen to make that change. These feelings can range from anxiety, anger and threat at one extreme to excitement, satisfaction and happiness at the other. One thing is sure, if you ignore people's feelings about any change required by an assignment, you do so at your peril. To handle this you need a number of skills related to helping people acknowledge, explore and come to terms with their feelings.

Dealing with your own feelings   You will not be able to help other people deal with their feelings if you find it difficult to deal with your own. You need to be in touch with your own feelings because those feelings can tell you a lot about what is going on around you. If you are uncomfortable and anxious it is likely that others will be too. If you can talk about your feelings it makes it more legitimate for others to share theirs.

So what skills do you require if you are to operate effectively in each of these seven areas? We have listed all those we think are important in each category as Checklist 3.1 at the end of the chapter. Before turning to our checklist, write down all the skills you think are important in each category, then compare your list with ours.

Skills I require to know myself adequately

-
-
-
-
-
-

Skills I need to communicate with groups and individuals

-
-

-
-
-
-

Observation and feedback skills I require

-
-
-
-
-
-

Skills I need to help groups solve problems and make decisions

-
-
-
-
-
-

Skills I require to facilitate team building

-
-
-
-
-
-

Skills I need to help people deal with their feelings

-
-
-
-
-
-

Skills I need to deal with my own feelings

-
-
-
-
-
-

When you compare your checklist with ours, add any of your own items that you feel we have missed. Then examine yourself critically against each item on the checklist and identify which skills you feel proficient in, which you should work on and develop and which you overuse and could use less often.

It is impossible to go into detail here about all the individual interpersonal skills noted in the checklist. That would be the subject of a complete book in itself. We can, however, take some of the principal skills and look at the barriers which prevent people from developing or using them and then look at ways you can start to develop them for yourself.

What prevents me from using these skills?

We have already pointed out that many of the basic interpersonal skills that you require to manage relationships with your clients are fairly simple. You probably learned many of them quite naturally as a child and then somewhere along the line you unlearned them. Children, for example, have little difficulty saying how they feel. By the time they become adults, however, many of them find this very difficult.

So what prevents you from using these skills? Inherent in this question lies the key to personal development. If you can identify the barriers that prevent you from listening effectively or asserting your rights, then you can start to develop a strategy for removing those barriers.

To help you start to think through some of your own barriers to personal development we have chosen a few of the key skills from the checklist for individual development (Checklist 3.1). For each skill we will ask you to:

- Identify the possible barriers that prevent people doing that activity effectively, then compare your list with ours.
- Identify those barriers which particularly apply to you.
- Identify ways of overcoming each of the barriers.

The skills we have chosen are:

- Asking others to comment on your behaviour
- Listening
- Observing what happens in a group
- Dealing with feelings

Asking others to comment on your behaviour

If you are to be aware of your strengths and weaknesses it is important that you are able to solicit feedback on your behaviour from others. This may be very difficult and most of us are probably uncertain of how we are seen by our colleagues, subordinates and clients. Write down as many barriers as you can to soliciting feedback and then compare your list with ours below.

Some of the barriers to soliciting feedback from others are:

- Fear that they will focus only on weaknesses
- They may tell me things I did not know about
- I might get information I am not ready for
- I might feel hurt by what is said
- I am even more uncomfortable with compliments
- I might be seen as 'fishing for compliments'
- The other person might be embarrassed at being asked

Table 3.1 *Soliciting feedback*

My barriers to soliciting feedback	Strategies for overcoming them

Table 3.2 *Some strategies for overcoming barriers to soliciting feedback*

Barriers to soliciting feedback	Ways of overcoming them
Fears about getting painful negative information	• Start by asking specific questions about safe areas • Ask for some positive and some negative feedback • Only ask for feedback from people you know genuinely value you • Give yourself time to talk through any hurt you might feel, but don't blame the other person
Fears about the other person's reaction, e.g. • Not sure how the other person will react • Might embarrass the other person • Not sure that I will get the truth	• Choose someone with whom you have a formal relationship where feedback can be seen as a normal part of that relationship, e.g. your boss, a regular client, a subordinate • Choose a close friend • Contract with a colleague to give each other honest positive and negative feedback on a regular basis
Unable to deal with positive feedback and compliments	• Practise by acknowledging to yourself when you've done something well • Write down a list of all the things you're good at • Write down a list of things you like about yourself

- The request for feedback might be seen as insecurity or weakness
- I am not sure I will get the truth

Doubtless you have identified barriers that we haven't. Now you should go back over both lists and identify those barriers which most apply to you. Write these down in Table 3.1 and then identify ways you can work on removing each barrier. In Table 3.2 we have selected a number of barriers and identified strategies for removing them.

Listening   Listening is perhaps the single most important skill of the client-centred consultant. Gaining entry with the client and really crystallizing the nature of the problem demands a high level of listening skills. Often simply listening as people pour out their troubles or think through what they will do next is extremely helpful. Listening ought to be easy, we all have two ears, yet it is actually very difficult. Probably the reason for the difficulty is that there are so many barriers to effective listening. Write down as many as you can, then compare your list with ours below.

Barriers to effective listening include:

- Thinking of other things
- Being distracted by emotive words
- Disagreeing with the other person
- Listening for flaws in the other person's argument
- Wanting to express own thoughts and views
- Prejudice
- Assuming that you won't understand
- Lack of interest
- Interpreting and distorting what has been said
- Outside distractions
- Not valuing the person being listened to

As before, compare your list with ours. Now identify those listening barriers which apply to you; list them in Table 3.3 and for each one identify ways you can overcome the barrier. In Table 3.4 we have selected a number of listening barriers and identified strategies for overcoming them.

Table 3.3 *Listening barriers*

My listening barriers	Ways I can overcome them

Table 3.4   Strategies for overcoming listening blockages

Listening blockages	Ways of overcoming them
Outside distractions	• Find somewhere quiet • Try to remove them • Really concentrate on what the client is saying
• Disagreeing with the other person • Own thoughts and opinions	• Be open-minded • Don't judge • Try to understand why the client has a different opinion to yours • Remember, you might learn something new
• Distraction of own thoughts • Mind wandering off onto other things • Emotional trigger words which always produce a response in you	• Make mental summaries of what the client says • Make notes if possible • Be attentive • Be aware of the words and ideas which trigger off an emotional reaction in you. Work at responding more neutrally to them
Interpretation and distortion	• Check your understanding of what your client has said • Reflect back the main ideas • Summarize

Observing what happens in a group

When you are collecting data you will need not only to identify the technical aspects of the problem but also to be aware of how people's behaviour, and the way they interact with each other, impinges on the

Table 3.5   Observing groups

My barriers to observing groups	Ways I might overcome them

Table 3.6 *Strategies for overcoming barriers to using observation skills*

Barriers to observation	Ways of overcoming them
Focusing on the content, e.g. • Getting over-involved in the discussion • Listening to *what* is said, not *how* it is said	• Remind yourself that your role is to observe, not take part • Consciously take time out of meetings when you don't participate in discussions but observe how people are behaving
Unable to structure your observations, e.g. • Don't know what to look for • Don't know what is important • The sheer volume of the data	• Use the observation sheets provided at the end of Chapter 7
Making judgements about what is happening	• Try not to look for right or wrong behaviour. Identify what happens and let others decide if it's appropriate: e.g. if one person in a group speaks six times more than anyone else, this is not in itself right or wrong, but it may be significant and helpful to the group to point it out
The lack of clarity, e.g. • Fear of getting it wrong • The ambiguity and uncertainty	• Accept that there is so much happening you can't observe everything • Let the group decide what to do with the data you have gathered • Practise

problem. You need to be able to step back from the group, and observe what is going on. Again, this is more difficult than it sounds. So what do you think are the main barriers to using observation skills? List as many as you can think of, then compare them with our list below.

Barriers to observing groups of people working together include:

• Getting over-involved in the discussion
• Listening to *what* is said rather than *how* it is said
• Not knowing what to look for
• Not knowing what is important and what is not
• Making judgements about what is happening
• The sheer volume of data
• The ambiguity and lack of certainty about what is taking place
• It is often difficult to quantify the observation
• Fear of 'getting it wrong'

What are the factors that prevent you from observing groups as well as you might? List them in Table 3.5 and then try to identify ways of overcoming them for yourself. In Table 3.6 we have selected a number of barriers to develop observation skills and for each barrier identified strategies for overcoming them.

Dealing with feelings

As a client-centred consultant you will constantly be working in the realm of feelings. Your clients may welcome you or be suspicious of you; they may welcome change or feel threatened by it; they may be stimulated and motivated by the style of the manager or feel frustrated and undervalued by it. People never feel neutral and whatever feelings they have will influence their behaviour. Without the skills to acknowledge, explore and deal with your clients' feelings you can't work in a client-centred way. So what are the barriers which prevent consultants dealing sensitively with their clients' feelings? List as many barriers as you can think of and then compare them with our list below.

There are numerous barriers that make it difficult to deal with feelings. Many of these relate to the way feelings are dealt with in the family, in organizations and in our culture as a whole. Some of them include:

- It is difficult to acknowledge our own feelings
- Thoughts and ideas are valued, feelings and emotions are not
- We confuse thoughts with feelings
- I am afraid the other person might get annoyed if asked about feelings
- Feelings are personal and private
- Asking about feelings feels false and contrived
- Feelings are dangerous
- I am afraid I might not be able to cope
- I might get out of my depth
- Things might get out of control
- I feel uncomfortable and awkward when others are emotional

Now list in Table 3.7 the barriers which apply to you and again try to identify strategies for dealing with each barrier. In Table 3.8 we have selected a number of barriers and again identified a number of ways to alleviate each one.

Table 3.7   Dealing with feelings

My barriers to dealing with feelings	Ways I might overcome them

Table 3.8 *Strategies for overcoming barriers to dealing with feelings*

Barriers to dealing with feelings	Ways of overcoming them
Lack of awareness of my own feelings, e.g. • Difficulty acknowledging my own feelings • I have been taught to value thoughts and ideas	• Make a list of all the things you enjoy doing and how you feel when you do them • Identify a past or current project and write down how you would like your clients to feel at the end. How did they feel? • Practise sharing feelings in a safe environment
Not knowing how people will react to being asked about feelings, e.g. • Feelings are personal and private • Asking about feelings is false and contrived • I am afraid the other person might get annoyed if I ask about feelings	• Ask yourself 'Are all feelings private?' • Try it. Ask questions like 'You have told me about the problem—how does it feel?' • Try to be sensitive to how people are feeling. Check out if you are right by saying: 'That seems to make you angry' 'You seem to be really looking forward to that' 'You really seem to have enjoyed that'
Fears, e.g. • Feelings are dangerous • I can't control them • I might get out of my depth	• Remember, it is a long road between asking someone how they feel and mental breakdown • You don't need to be a psychiatrist to deal with the majority of people's feelings— just a sensitive listener

Summary   Here we have only been able to examine in detail the barriers to using a small number of skills listed in the checklist for individual development (Checklist 3.1). The approach, however, is valid for developing any of the skills. First, identify the skill you want to develop or the behaviour you'd like to do more of. Then list the barriers that prevent you from utilizing that skill. Finally, develop a strategy for overcoming those barriers.

How can I develop the skills?

The first thing to say about developing skills is that there is no panacea, no instant button to press that will transform you into a paragon of that particular virtue. Building interpersonal skills always requires some change in behaviour and that means first of all unlearning current ingrained behaviour. As we have seen, there are often psychological barriers that make it difficult to use certain behaviours.

So where do you start? The first thing to do is to set yourself reasonable targets. Don't start by selecting thirty items from the personal development checklist and deciding to work on them all. It's much better to be working on a maximum of three or four at any one time.

If you are planning to change behaviour you can see it as a consulting assignment in which you are both client and consultant. If you are planning to use the consulting cycle with your clients, then you ought to be able to use it on yourself. To make things simpler we'll assume, throughout the following section, that you've decided to try to improve your listening skills. But first let us remind ourselves of the phases in the consulting cycle, as shown in Figure 3.1

Collecting data about current behaviour

We start at this phase because as you're both client and consultant in this assignment we can assume a high level of entry and you've already made a contract with yourself to work on this particular aspect of your behaviour.

The first thing to do is to get a picture of how you operate at the moment. You probably already have a good idea of the aspects of listening you're good at and what needs to be improved. Ask yourself what is preventing you from making the desired change. How do you feel about your current way of listening? What are the pay-offs for your current behaviour? It is always useful to get feedback from other people about your current behaviour. No matter how self-aware you are you

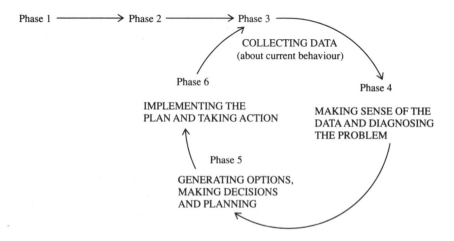

Figure 3.1 *The phases of the consulting cycle*

can't see yourself as others do. You may well be over-critical of yourself or unaware that the piece of behaviour is a symptom of a bigger problem that only others can see.

Another way of gathering data about your current behaviour is to practise the skill by doing experiential learning activities. There are a number of these outlined briefly at the end of this chapter.

Making sense of the data
You may now need to put the data you have collected about yourself into some kind of context. You may want to watch other people, good listeners, and observe how their listening style is different from your own. It may be helpful to read an article on effective listening skills to clarify how your own style differs from the ideal.

Options, decisions and planning
You now need to plan a strategy for working on the new behaviour. You need to ask questions such as:

- What precisely will I be doing when I am using this skill effectively?
- What barriers will make it difficult?
- How long will it take me to become proficient?
- What are the steps along the way?
- What situations will be available to practise?
- What help do I need from other people?
- How will I ask for that help?
- How will I know if I am succeeding?
- How will I get feedback?
- Where and when am I going to start?

These questions have been reproduced as Checklist 3.2 at the end of this chapter. By answering them you should have a clear plan of action.

Implementation
You now need to put your plan into action and take as many opportunities to practise the new behaviour as you can. Of course, the model is cyclical and as you practise you need to gather more data about how successful you've been and how close to your own description of 'proficient' you are.

Summary

- To be a client-centred consultant you need a high level of interpersonal skills if you are to be successful in managing relationships with your clients and helping them to work together more effectively. This skill can be divided into seven categories:
  - knowing myself
  - communication skills
  - observation and feedback skills
  - helping client groups solve problems and make decisions
  - team-building skills
  - dealing with people's feelings
  - dealing with my own feelings
- The first step in skill building is to identify the psychological barriers

to using that behaviour. You can then work out a strategy for over-coming the barriers.
- When working on developing any skill you need to:
  - find out how you do it now
  - work out a strategy for using the new behaviour
  - get feedback to tell you how successful you are being in using the new behaviour

Exercises

1 Using friends

Purpose   To increase self-awareness.
Make a list of those areas of your behaviour which you feel you would like more information about. Select someone you know and value and ask for direct and honest feedback. You may be able to contract to offer feedback to each other as a reciprocal arrangement. If you do this, make sure you don't collude simply to be 'nice' to each other.

2 Sandwich boards

Purpose   To get positive and negative feedback in a training group.
Participants in a group are invited to take two sheets of flip-chart paper each. These are attached to each participant with sellotape so that one sheet hangs down over the participant's front and one at the back.

Each member then takes a flip chart and the group mills around and writes feedback comments on everyone's sheets. The basic rule is that everyone should add one piece of feedback to the front and one to the back of everyone else. The feedback on each participant's back should be positive and value the person. Conversely, the front sheets should be filled with aspects of that individual's *behaviour* which could usefully be developed.

Once all sheets are complete the group reconvenes. Then time must be given for each person to talk through the comments received, in partic-ular how each feels about having received them.

3 Our gift to you

Purpose   To give and receive feedback on consulting skills within a group of consultants.
This exercise is designed to help consultants get feedback from other members of a team within which they have been working. This could be a group of people who work together, or have worked together on an assignment or training programme. It is an exercise which must be handled with care and requires a skilled facilitator to ensure that the following prerequisites are met:

- There must be an open, trusting climate within the group.
- There should be a high level of care and desire to help each other.
- People must feel valued by other group members.
- Group members should already have started to give each other some feedback.

- Everyone should want to do the exercise.
- A high level of honesty is essential.

The way you do the exercise is as follows:

(a) Each person spends 15–20 minutes alone thinking about each member of the team and how each behaves as a consultant.

(b) The team re-forms, without the facilitator, and all the names are put in the pot. They take out one at a time to determine the order in which feedback will be given. They should not pull all the names out at the beginning or the pressure on the last person becomes a form of 'creeping death'. The Russian roulette method is good— someone selects the first name and that person, after receiving feedback, pulls out the next name, and so on.

(c) For 10 minutes (no more/no less) the person receiving the feedback stands at the flip chart ready to write. The rest of the group provide feedback by giving adjectives—words or phrases—that describe that person. Recipients can divide the sheet into plus and minus columns and decide on which side to put the words, but they may not comment—only write.

(d) The recipient leaves the words on the flip chart so that the group can see them and hands in their Personal Feedback Sheet to a member of the group, who will coordinate its completion. This sheet has several sections. They overlap to some extent but all are important and all should be completed.

Our gift to you
Personal Feedback Sheet

To _____

The things we have found most valuable about you are:

Your major strengths as a consultant are:

Your most helpful actions in this group have been:

Your principal weaknesses as a consultant are:

The types of behaviour you might think of changing are:

From _____   Date _____

The person receiving the feedback now sits outside the group but inside the room listening to the discussion as the group decides what to write. The recipient may find it useful to make notes of the discussion while listening. This discussion and completion of the 'gift' should take 20 minutes—any shorter time is likely to be superficial; any longer and the group could be 'sawing sawdust'.

When members of the group have agreed what they want to say, their comments are written on the feedback sheet. All members sign it (very important) and it is given to the person concerned. (NB This is not a consensus exercise—if one or two group members think an aspect is important, it should be put down.)

(e) The person receiving the feedback then has up to 10 minutes to ask for clarification or explanation of either the adjectives on the flip chart, or the feedback sheet. Recipients should use this time to make sure they really understand the feedback given—especially behaviour they might think of changing.

4 A letter to myself

Purpose Planning for increased personal effectiveness.
This exercise is long-term and is a variation of one used by the Brontë sisters. Most organizations now have some form of annual appraisal. Why not use a variation of this purely for yourself? At the time of your appraisal (or new year, or your birthday) write a letter to yourself describing:

- your strengths
- your weaknesses
- your hopes and fears
- areas you wish to develop over the next year (most important of all).

As the letter will only be read by you, you can afford to be brutally honest. When complete, seal it in an envelope and file it away until next year. When the next year comes around (and that will be quicker than you think) don't start your next personal appraisal until you have read what you wrote last year. We suspect you will be amazed how much you have changed.

5 Listening and summarizing

Purpose To practise listening and summarizing skills.
If you have a TV and video recorder then try listening to, and recording, the evening news broadcast. Most stations now adopt a three-part pattern:

1 They announce the headlines.
2 They give you the news.
3 Finally, they summarize the main points of the news once again.

You can use this to develop your listening and summarizing skills. Switch on your TV and video at the start of the news. Listen to, and record the programme. As they start the summary at the end, switch off the TV and make your own summary of what has been said. Try to summarize the points you have heard. In the meantime your video will have captured the summary announced on TV. Finally, rewind your video and replay the recording. At the same time check the TV summary against your own. It will highlight what you listened to and remembered, measured against the main points that the broadcasters felt were important.

6 Asking questions

Purpose   To practise asking open questions.

This exercise requires the help of a colleague. It is competitive and should be treated as fun. Each of you will take turns at being a speaker or a questioner for a fixed period of time in each role (say 5 minutes). Instructions for what to do in each role are given below.

Speaker

When you are the speaker, choose a topic to talk about (e.g. a holiday, film, favourite interest, sport) and tell your questioner your chosen topic. Your questioner will then ask you questions on the topic. If he or she asks an open question (i.e. begining with who, what, why, where, when or how) give some information. If he or she asks a closed question, answer with yes or no (do be quite ruthless where you can answer yes or no). You score a point whenever you answer yes or no.

Questioner

When you are the questioner it is your job to ask questions. If you ask an open question and receive a piece of information, you score a point. If you ask a closed question and receive a yes or no, the speaker scores a point.

Example

Questioner:	Where did you go on holiday?
Speaker:	Spain (Questioner scores a point)
Questioner:	Did you like it?
Speaker:	Yes (Speaker scores a point)
Questioner:	How did you get there.
Speaker:	By plane (Questioner scores a point)

And so on for 5 minutes.

When you have both had a go at each role, total up your points. Whoever scores the most wins the round.

7 Observing people

Purpose   To practise observation skills.

This exercise is best carried out in a pair or in a small group. However many of you choose to participate, start by agreeing on some material to observe—say 10 or 15 minutes from a video or 'soap' on TV—watch the programme and each of you make your own observation notes (or use one of the instruments in Chapter 7). At the end of the allotted observation time share your observations with your colleagues and check one another's accuracy. As a variation you might like to choose some specific behaviours for observation practice, e.g.:

- non-verbal behaviour
- eye contact
- mannerisms
- asking questions
- building on one another's comments.

NB This exercise is best carried out with recorded material. If there is any disagreement you can then replay the recording to check your data.

8 Observing groups

Purpose   To practise observing groups and giving feedback.
This exercise requires you to ask a group of people who are having a meeting if they will allow you to observe their behaviour. This might be part of a normal meeting at work or a group working for some other purpose. Agree with the group that you will observe for 15–30 minutes and then give feedback. Sit outside the group so that you don't participate in the discussion.

Try not to pay attention to the content of the discussion, rather observe how people are working together. You may use the observation sheets at the end of Chapter 7.

At the end of the discussion period share your observations with the group and ask how these compare with their observations of what was happening. Try to make your observations as objective as possible without evaluating any of the behaviour you saw.

Make sure you get feedback from the group on which of your observations were helpful and which were not.

9 Problem solving and decision making

Purpose   To practise problem-solving and decision-making techniques.
Select a current difficulty or problem you are experiencing at work. Apply one of the problem-solving techniques described in Chapter 7 (e.g. decision trees or force field analysis). If you apply the technique rigorously you will probably find it helps you to find a way forward.

10 Identifying feelings

Purpose   To extend the vocabulary people have to describe feelings. Working individually or as a group write down as many words to describe feelings and emotions as you can. Ensure that every word is a genuine feeling. It should be possible to generate a list of over 100 words.

11 Exploring feelings

Purpose   To practise exploring other people's feelings.
Working as a pair, one person volunteers to be the client and the other the consultant. The client should choose a real problem that he or she has at present. It can be from work or outside work; the only prerequisite is that it is genuine.

The client should talk about the problem. The consultant should listen and help the client explore his or her feelings about the problem. The consultant can only ask questions about the client's feelings. It may be necessary to ask a 'feelings' question more than once if the client gives a thought or opinion as an answer.

The consultation should last for about 15 minutes. At the end of this time client and consultant should discuss fully how they both felt during the exercise.

Repeat the exercise so that each person is able to experience both roles.

Checklist 3.1 *Consulting skills—a checklist for individual development*

This checklist is designed to help you identify the skills you require to be a successful client-centred consultant. It is intended to help you recognize the range of skills you require and identify those which you need to work on.

Read through the list of skills and for each one identify whether:

- You are already competent in this activity and use the skill appropriately.
- This is a skill that you need to develop or one you underuse at the moment.
- This is a skill you are competent in but actually overuse at the moment so that you become less effective. You need to work on doing less of this activity.

	Competent	Need to develop	Need to do less
Knowing myself			
1 Understanding how I am seen by others	....	....	....
2 Being aware of how my personal style differs from others	....	....	....
3 Being able to ask others to comment on my behaviour	....	....	....
4 Being able to assess my own strengths and weaknesses	....	....	....
5 Being able to set goals for personal change	....	....	....
6 Being able to work on improving personal effectivenesss	....	....	....
7	....	....	....
8	....	....	....
9	....	....	....
10	....	....	....

	Competent	Need to develop	Need to do less

Communication skills

		Competent	Need to develop	Need to do less
11	Talking in small groups	....	....	....
12	Talking in large groups	....	....	....
13	Asking questions	....	....	....
14	Drawing others out	....	....	....
15	Summarizing and clarifying others' ideas	....	....	....
16	Building on others' contributions	....	....	....
17	Listening	....	....	....
18	Keeping to the topic	....	....	....
19	Summarizing the discussion	....	....	....
20	Showing interest	....	....	....
21	Dealing with more senior people	....	....	....
22	Asserting my own rights	....	....	....
23	Stating my own needs	....	....	....
24		....	....	....
25		....	....	....

Observation and feedback skills

		Competent	Need to develop	Need to do less
26	Being aware of high and low participators	....	....	....
27	Noting if people are excluded	....	....	....
28	Recognizing who talks to whom	....	....	....
29	Noting how decisions are made	....	....	....
30	Being aware of who takes on leadership roles	....	....	....
31	Being sensitive to how people in the group are feeling	....	....	....
32	Sensing tension in the group	....	....	....
33	Being aware of how open or closed the group is	....	....	....
34	Identifying those issues which are avoided	....	....	....
35	Giving feedback on behaviour in the group	....	....	....
36	Giving feedback to individuals	....	....	....
37		....	....	....
38		....	....	....
39		....	....	....
40		....	....	....

	Competent	Need to develop	Need to do less

Helping client groups solve problems and make decisions

41	Identifying and clarifying goals and objectives	....	....	....
42	Clearly defining the problem under discussion	....	....	....
43	Examining all facets of the problem	....	....	....
44	Exploring human aspects of the problem	....	....	....
45	Surfacing vested interests and feelings about the problem	....	....	....
46	Encouraging others to generate ideas	....	....	....
47	Creativity—developing new ideas	....	....	....
48	Evaluating options	....	....	....
49	Helping groups make decisions	....	....	....
50	Helping groups explore their commitment to decisions made	....	....	....
51	Encouraging groups to develop action plans	....	....	....
52		....	....	....
53		....	....	....
54		....	....	....
55		....	....	....

Team building

56	Helping the team to confront difficult issues	....	....	....
57	Drawing attention to unhelpful behaviour	....	....	....
58	Dealing with tension	....	....	....
59	Helping the team deal with conflict	....	....	....
60	Giving praise and appreciation	....	....	....
61	Supporting individuals against group pressure	....	....	....
62	Helping team members acknowledge each other's strengths	....	....	....
63	Helping team members give each other feedback	....	....	....
64	Facilitating team review and critique	....	....	....
65		....	....	....

	Competent	Need to develop	Need to do less

Dealing with people's feelings

	Competent	Need to develop	Need to do less
66 Being sensitive to others' feelings	....	....	....
67 Asking people how they feel	....	....	....
68 Acknowledging people's feelings	....	....	....
69 Helping others express their feelings	....	....	....
70 Being comfortable with close-ness and affection	....	....	....
71 Facing conflict and anger	....	....	....
72 Dealing with hostility and suspicion	....	....	....
73 Withstanding silences	....	....	....
74	....	....	....
75	....	....	....

Dealing with my own feelings

	Competent	Need to develop	Need to do less
76 Being aware of my own feelings	....	....	....
77 Being able to identify my feelings	....	....	....
78 Expressing my feelings to others	....	....	....
79 Expressing the following feelings:			
• Warmth	....	....	....
• Affection	....	....	....
• Comfort	....	....	....
• Discomfort	....	....	....
• Anxiety	....	....	....
• Frustration	....	....	....
• Fear	....	....	....
• Confidence	....	....	....
• Uncertainty	....	....	....
• Irritation	....	....	....
• Annoyance	....	....	....
• Anger	....	....	....
• Gratitude	....	....	....
• Satisfaction	....	....	....
• Excitement	....	....	....
• Determination	....	....	....
others •	....	....	....
•	....	....	....
•	....	....	....
•	....	....	....

Checklist 3.2 *Planning new behaviour*

1 What new behaviour or new skill do I want to work on?

2 What precisely will I be doing when I am using that skill effectively?

3 How does that differ from the way I operate now?

4 What barriers to changed behaviour will I need to overcome?

5 How long will it take me to become proficient?

6 What are the steps along the way?

7 What situations will be available to practise?

8 What help do I need from other people? Who?

9 How will I ask for that help?

10 How will I know if I am succeeding?

11 How will I get feedback?

12 Where and when am I going to start?

4 Starting the consultation

Initial steps   The question of what to do at the start of a consultation is probably best answered from the client's point of view, i.e. what types of questions will be framed by the client who sits awaiting the arrival of the consultant? However, for the present let us consider the case of the willing participant. It is at this point that people ask if it matters that the person you first see is not the real client. Our answer is usually that you have to gain entry before you can find out!

Exercise 1
Try to generate a list of questions which your client may be thinking about prior to your arrival. Here are three to get you started:

- Will I like the consultant?
- Will he/she like me?
- How will he/she treat me?

When you have finished turn to Checklist 4.1 at the end of the chapter and check your list against ours. From the two lists you can probably get a fair view of the client's concerns at the start of a consultation; it follows therefore that you had better start to address some of these before you go any further. When we look back at some of our disasters we can usually point to either an inferior contract or more importantly insufficient time spent at the start on building a relationship. This is what the initial stage is all about.

In Chapter 1 we mentioned that a consultant needs a positive self-image and enough self-confidence, skill and ability to retain it in the face of adversity. It follows that at the start you should spend some time on your own self-image. Assuming that the initial contact by telephone or letter was appropriate and has not queered the pitch before you arrive, then it is important to make a good first impression. You will have made sure that you are appropriately dressed, have all your information at your finger tips, have arrived at the right place at the right time and know whom you are to meet. However, all this is rarely enough; you also need to deal with how you feel. Depending upon your particular orientation this part of preparation is usually called grounding or centring. It means getting yourself into a frame of mind to meet your client and deal with any difficulties which may arise while at the same time retaining your self-control.

Preparing to meet clients

Meeting your clients for the first time can be a stressful occasion. You are likely to be on unfamiliar territory; this can be just as true if you are visiting someone in the next department as it is when calling on a geographically distant associate company.

The initial contact with your client or client group is likely to give rise to all sorts of impressions which may or may not be favourable. So it is important to give some attention to your own needs before you meet. Although you can do little to influence the feelings of your client before you meet (remember the list of questions you compiled in the previous exercise) at least you can assess your own physical and mental condition and get in touch with your feelings. This assessment is concerned with centring or grounding so that nothing knocks you off balance. Tom Crum in his delightful book, *Magic of Conflict* (1989), describes centring as a state 'when the mind, body and spirit become fully integrated in dynamic balance and connectedness with the world around us. There is a heightened awareness and sensitivity, a feeling that everything is perfect the way it is. The truth of who we are as human beings is revealed.' This might be rather much for mere mortal consultants, but there seems little doubt that to get as near to this as possible would be a good state to achieve before meeting your client.

To do this you can ensure that you arrive for the meeting in plenty of time; you can then spend a few minutes on your own, becoming aware of your heart rate (is it normal or speeded up?), your breathing (is it fast and shallow?), your muscle tension (in your arms, shoulders or where else?), is your mouth dry and you feel that talking is like spitting feathers? Being aware of these symptoms allows you to do something about them. First you can deal directly with the physical symptoms— take deep breaths, tense and then relax your hands, arms or shoulders to reduce the tension, get a drink of water, and so on. The second action you can take is to ask yourself why these symptoms are present. What wild fantasies are giving rise to these fears and concerns? What unattainable goals have you set yourself? What are your worst fears about the assignment or meeting? By thinking through some of these you will help yourself to make a more realistic assessment of the outcomes of the encounter. Finally, you should be able to meet your client without showing the tensions you may feel inside. You will be grounded and little will be able to knock you off balance. The next step is to think through some of the issues that are around when you meet the client so that the meeting is purposeful and meets the needs of both of you.

A purposeful initial meeting

Let us assume that you have decided that the main purpose when you meet the client is to achieve a meeting of minds and to begin to establish some trust between you. It is likely that this will best be generated by trying to establish a collaborative relationship. First this allows you to be client-centred and share the responsibility for the success of the intervention and secondly you are, whether you like it or not, a role model for your client. If you talk one way and act differently then the client is likely to be confused. Your first impressions of the client are important but they must not be allowed to colour your judgement or your behaviour. It is very easy to dislike clients on sight and then look for evidence to support your theory. Likewise it is possible to view your clients in a favourable light, assuming that their intentions are honourable even when their behaviour leaves something to be desired. As a consequence you start looking for evidence to support that theory instead!

From our experience there are four situations that can be thought through before meeting a potential client. We say 'potential' client because you have to accept that the person you see at the start may not be the real client (or may be only one part of the total client system). However, for the purposes of gaining entry, you must assume that you have at least a potential client. The penalty for assuming that your contact is not part of the system is that you may be inclined to skimp on this phase only to find out later that he or she is indeed the client. The safest course seems to be to assume that your contact is part of the client system and go from there. If you find out later that you have to gain entry with other parts of the client system as well, then what have you lost?

The four situations which may arise are as follows:

A You have been in the department before with that client or with another client.

X You have been invited by the people with the problem.

B This is your first ever visit to the department or with this person.

Y You have been imposed by a person with power and you may or may not be welcome.

Situation A with X.   The danger will probably be obvious. If you know the people and have been invited to help you may feel that you do not have to bother gaining entry. However, even if you have worked with a particular client or client system as recently as a week ago it is vital to check out what has happened in the meantime. As an internal consultant you are quite likely to know about significant changes affecting the organization or your client's part of it, but it is still worth checking in case you have been kept in the dark or you know something your client doesn't. If there have been significant changes in the client's private life you may want to check whether or not these are likely to affect his or her behaviour or mental attitude at work. It will be very surprising if they don't. Allowing the client space and time to discuss such issues may well be enough. You might also need to decide whether or not to check with other people who know your client. The culture, norms and standards of the organization will usually tell you how far to go.

Situation B with X.   If this is your first visit it is likely that you will have to spend some time building a relationship with the person who is your initial contact. Bearing in mind what we said earlier about making assumptions about real clients, you will need to gain entry to check whether this is the case here. As an internal consultant you may be in a less favourable position than an external consultant; clients often find it easier to admit and share problems with an outsider. For example, company training officers often find it difficult to get participants to share real problems on courses where everyone is from the same department or organization. On public courses where participants are usually the only representative from their organization this is usually much less of a problem. However, as we discussed in Chapter 1, internal consultants usually have many distinct advantages which can work in their favour.

If you have been invited in by the people who have the problem or want something done about it, you are halfway home before you start. You will still have to establish whether or not you can help but the difficulty is more likely to be a different one in our experience. What often happens is that you are not allowed time for gaining entry as the client meets you with 'I'm glad you could come—let me tell you about the problem'. You find yourself rushed headlong into data collection before you even have a contract! So it may well be important to let the client tell you about the problem while you gently probe for information that will help you build a relationship. Questions which somehow take the client back to the beginning may be useful: 'How did the problem come to your notice?', 'Who is involved in the problem?', 'What effect is the problem having on you and the department?' Other questions which focus on how the problem is managed might help: 'How do you feel about the problem?', 'Who else is worried about the problem?', 'What happens when problems come up?', 'Who are the key people involved and how do they feel?', 'How have you managed similar problems in the past?'. Above all, you need to keep your attention on what the client is telling you about the problem while at the same time listening for what the client is not telling you. We will deal with collecting data in Chapter 5 but it is important at this stage to be aware of all the data there is around. Your ears are important in picking up the way the client talks to you and other people as well as what is being said. Your eyes will tell you a lot about the environment, the layout, the furnishing, and the differences attributable to status. You will be able to feel whether the place is a warm or cold place to work in—and this has nothing to do with the central heating or air conditioning! And your intuition should be working overtime during the gaining entry phase. All this is especially important if you are on your first visit.

Situation A or B with Y. If you have been imposed on the client system you will probably have a difficult task just gaining entry. It may make some difference if you have been to the department before, but your main difficulty is likely to be one of non-cooperation and a great reluctance to tell you anything. Before you can start to make any sense of the situation you will probably have to deal with the bad feelings or anger which is around and which may or may not be expressed verbally. It is your job to get these bad feelings into the open so that you can help your client deal with them. If they are not being expressed you may have to indicate how the situation feels to you by saying something like 'I feel very uncomfortable here. There seems to be some unexpressed hostility to me being here. Is that right?' You may well have to listen for some time while the clients play a game of 'ain't it awful', saying what they think and feel and inviting you to collude. Your job is to stay out of the game, stay calm and let the emotion surface. Remember no clients are able to deal logically with a problem while they are emotionally charged. An acceptant style will enable you to remain neutral, be empathic but not take sides, and let the client know that you understand and genuinely want to help.

There is still one more important aspect of gaining entry to keep in mind. While the main objective is for you to gain entry with the client it is also important that the client gains entry with you. Remembering all the questions that may be going through the client's mind before you arrive (as discussed in Exercise 1) can help you steer the gaining entry phase so that you get the client to surface some of the questions, or you may answer them even though they have not been voiced. It is also important that you have given some thought to what you want the client to know about you before you start. It is our experience that clients often see gaining entry as a waste of time given over to social chit-chat. However, without getting into an argument, it is vital to ensure that both you and the client gain enough entry with each other to get a valid contract. You can do this by listening actively and picking up on similar backgrounds, shared values and feelings, similar experiences or interests which will give you the opportunities you need. If the meeting is in the client's office you may gain quite a lot from observing how the office is furnished or arranged, what hangs on the walls, what trophies are displayed and so on. Everything is grist to the mill for the consultant who wishes to gain entry effectively.

Exercise 2
From what you know and what you have read so far, try to make a list of all the reasons why gaining entry is important. Then compare it with Checklist 4.2 at the end of the chapter.

Barriers to gaining entry

The barriers to gaining entry are twofold—your needs and the clients' needs. Your needs play a part because it is quite hard to keep coming back to gaining entry issues when the clients are trying desperately to get into data collection and problem solving. It is quite easy to collude with their desire especially if you find gaining entry to be the phase that you like least. In some instances it may be necessary to confront the issue directly and explain to clients that you need to establish a relationship before you can be sure that the rest of the intervention will be successful. Client needs can also be a barrier to gaining entry because, as we have suggested, they see it as time wasting. They may see talking about the way the problem is managed and their feelings about it as idle gossip. Somehow this attitude also needs confronting and clients helped to understand your need to know about the problem and all that surrounds it.

Apart from that there are other obvious barriers and difficulties to gaining entry. Some of these will be to do with the place and the environment; some will be to do with how you both behave to one another, but all the remaining ones are likely to be embedded in feelings: issues of trust, previous relationships, status, cultural norms, confidentiality, etc.

Exercise 3
Try listing as many barriers as you can think of and then compare your list with Checklist 4.3 at the end of the chapter.

What can I do about them?

Generally, you are likely to be into gaining entry before you realize that some of the barriers exist. For example, imagine you are called to a meeting in the client's office and are given no choice about where you sit. Furthermore you may find that the meeting is attended by more people than you expected, leaving you feeling very uncomfortable. In such situations you may have to grin and bear it or take the first opportunity to express your concern and feelings about the situation. In taking any action you will have to weigh up any risk of not gaining as much entry as might otherwise be possible.

Other barriers can be minimized by preparation before you arrive. For example, you can research the history of your department's relationships with the client's department and so on. This is often a wise precaution if you are going on your first visit, but in our experience it can also lead to preconceptions which may work against you. On balance our recommendation is to go with an open mind, give your potential client unconditional positive regard and be ready to deal with any non-cooperation and defensiveness if it arises. If the barriers are really getting in the way of progress towards a valid contract then you may have to stick at it until such time as you feel sufficient barriers have been removed or reduced. Checklist 4.4 at the end of this chapter gives a list of aspects of your relationship with clients that you can affect directly.

Consequences of not gaining entry

The consequences of not gaining entry are quite severe. For a start you are unlikely to build a relationship based on trust. The consequences may be that you do not get the information you need to help the client solve the problem, or you are given misinformation or even disinformation. A few clients may actually tell you lies just to ensure that you fail. The main difficulty we have experienced is that you are never quite sure that what the client is telling you is the truth. The consequences of that will be obvious. If you are in a situation where you do not trust the client and the client does not trust you, you are likely to be treated with suspicion whatever you do. The client is likely to attribute to you ulterior motives which you have never had and never even considered.

Despite this, there are times when you just have to move on, knowing that the gaining entry is incomplete and that you may have to continue gaining entry as the assignment progresses. Indeed, if you are working with a large group you could get to the end of the project and find that there are some people with whom you never gained entry. The crucial decision is—have you gained sufficient entry to ensure you can enter into a meaningful contract?

Does the client really need help?

A large variety of problems and difficulties might cause a client to seek help from a consultant, and all are likely to be presented as genuine needs by the client. However, it is possible that some problems arise from objectives which are not about improving effectiveness. You may have a choice about whether to work with these stated needs or you may not. However, it is unlikely you will bring about much improvement or problem solving. Furthermore, many ethical issues are likely to arise for both the client and the consultant. Nevertheless, it could be that you have to choose to go along with these needs until such time as it becomes obvious that you can go no further, although it may not be easy to spot these somewhat spurious reasons for calling you in when you make a contract. If you are to be successful in helping clients to solve their problem it is important that they have genuine reasons for asking for help. They also need to have a readiness for change and a willingness to try more effective ways of operating. By less genuine reasons for calling you in we mean those reasons which, on the surface, may seem genuine but which give you an uneasy feeling that there are hidden agendas around. The reasons given for wanting help are not what they seem.

Exercise 4
Try to list as many genuine and less genuine reasons why clients may seek change as you can. When you have finished compare it with Checklist 4.5 at the end of the chapter.

When to make a contract

It is possible to work at gaining entry until both you and the client are satisfied that you have built a relationship that is complete. However, this might take a long time and generally you do not have the amount of time available. Furthermore, it might be rather boring if you did. What you need to ask yourself is 'Have I gained enough entry to get a valid workable contract?' If the answer is yes, then carry on to make a contract. If the answer is no, then you will need to spend more time on gaining entry until you can answer yes. There are, however, some indicators to tell you when enough is enough. For example:

- Is there any previous experience with this client or department which you can use as a guide?
- Do you feel able to raise anything you wish to raise with the client?
- Do you have any nagging doubts which you feel unable to surface?
- Are you colluding with the client by not raising issues you feel uncomfortable about?

- Do you think the client is avoiding discussing significant issues?
- Does the conversation feel open and honest?
- What does your intuition tell you about your mutual readiness to make a contract?

Gaining entry and contracting are, without doubt, two of the most ill-used aspects of consulting and, in our experience, whenever we have had failures they can nearly always be put down to missing out on one or the other or both. However, we believe that it is better to err on the side of going into contracting too early than too late. Too early and you can always go back or renegotiate the contract; too late and you risk alienating your client by seeming to procrastinate unduly. After all, you are there to help the client solve the problem not just to build a relationship or make a contract.

Summary

- Gaining entry is the process of building an effective relationship with your clients. Unless you have gained entry and established a relationship of mutual openness, trust and honesty, your clients are unlikely to be sufficiently open about the real problem. The result will be an unsatisfactory contract.
- In the early stages of a consulting assignment clients are likely to be suspicious or resentful of your presence, especially if they feel that you have been imposed on them.
- Meeting clients can be stressful for the consultant as well as the client. It is important to have a positive self-image. You need to spend time 'getting grounded' before meeting your clients.
- To build an effective working relationship with clients you need to be open, share some of your own feelings, and be absolutely genuine. If you are dishonest, exaggerate past successes or try to manipulate your clients, you will only succeed in reinforcing the barriers and increasing mistrust.

Checklist 4.1 *Questions going through the client's mind at the beginning of the assignment*

- Will I like the consultant?
- Will it be a man or a woman/old or young/black or white?
- How will they treat me?
- Will they like me?
- What will happen if I don't like them?
- What will happen if they don't like me?
- Will I have to admit that I have got a problem?
- What shall we talk about when the consultant arrives?
- How much does he or she know about the problem/me/the department/the division?
- Are they here to give me a solution or help me solve the problem?
- How will they operate? Will they know how I feel? Will they care how I feel?

- What will they do with any information I give them?
- How senior are they compared with me—more or less or the same?
- Can I trust them? Will they trust me?
- I know what I want from them but will they want anything special from me?
- Will they be like the last consultants we had from that team/department/group?
- What will they need in the way of support, resources, space, time, etc?
- How can I tell them I don't have a problem?
- How can I tell them it's really someone else's problem (boss/subordinate/another department/a colleague)?
- Will I ever be able to get rid of them?
- I wonder what my boss has told them about me?
- Will they want to know what I think of the boss/my colleagues/any other members of staff?
- What will happen if I don't like what they tell me to do?
- Will I be able to cover up what I have been doing for the last month/year?
- Will they help me to get the changes I have wanted for years?
- Who cares about them—they are only consultants!

Checklist 4.2 *Reasons why gaining entry is important*

- Understand something about the client as a person.
- Let the client get to know you.
- Lay the groundwork for trust.
- Achieve a meeting of minds.
- Enable the client to state clearly the need for help.
- Minimize resistance to change.
- Get some idea of the client's readiness for change.
- Find out something of the motive for calling you in.
- Establish rapport.
- Establish your credibility.
- Decide if you can help.
- Decide if you want to help (if you have an option to refuse).
- Start/develop a relationship on which to build.
- Establish common ground.
- Find out how welcome/unwelcome you are.
- Survey the surroundings.
- Get a feel for the place.
- Soak up the atmosphere.
- Help the client let off steam.
- Get some idea of how the problem is being managed.
- Get some idea of the size of the problem.
- Find out how urgent the solution is.

Checklist 4.3 *Barriers and difficulties in gaining entry*

- Bad first impressions—you of the client, the client of you.
- Your appearance, manner, style may be off-putting or contrary to the client's norms.
- You may not be what the client expected—male/female, black/white, etc.
- You turn up late or the client keeps you waiting.
- The client misses the appointment altogether.
- Previous relationships—personal or departmental—get in the way.
- You are senior to the client or the client is senior to you.
- The setting and surroundings are not conducive to gaining entry—not private, not comfortable, too formal, etc.
- Why you are there—invited or imposed.
- Cultural norms in the department about asking for help are antagonistic to you.
- You are seen as an outsider—and we don't trust strangers.
- You know what the problem is and the client doesn't.
- Confidentiality—can you and the client be trusted to keep it?
- Client may feel out of control, especially of his or her feelings.
- Information can be a source of power—telling you may weaken that power base.
- The client may think the problem can be solved without your help.
- Your intervention may be part of/contribute to the problem.
- Client doesn't actually need any help.
- You are worried that you can't meet the client's expectations.
- You have information about the client that you can't share for political reasons.
- The client has information which can't be shared with you for similar reasons.
- There are no genuine reasons for calling you in.
- The client is not ready to change or even contemplate change.
- One or both of you have hidden agendas.
- Assumptions about what you will do and how you will operate get in the way.
- We don't wash our dirty linen in public.
- You should be talking to someone above me/below me.
- It isn't really this department's problem.
- We are being blamed for someone else's mistakes.
- Every question you ask is met with an evasive answer.

Checklist 4.4 *Building a relationship with your clients*

- Be genuine and honest with your clients.
- Be open about your own feelings.
- Try to be a human being not a role.
- Share something of yourself.
- Share relevant information about previous successes without working too hard to impress.

- Take a genuine interest in your clients.
- Ask questions.
- Clarify and check your understanding of what clients are saying.
- Value your clients.
- Acknowledge the importance of clients' feelings.
- Help your clients to surface and talk about their concerns and reservations about your presence.
- Encourage open discussion about underlying problems affecting your working relationship with clients.
- Ensure that you and your department always present a professional image.

Checklist 4.5   *Genuine and less genuine motivations for change*

Compare it with your list and if you come up with any we haven't come across please let us know.

Genuine motivations for consultancy

- Real difficulty in getting the job done.
- Feeling that something is wrong but not sure what.
- Find out how well we are doing against the outside world or other departments.
- A need to be more effective or needing new skills: budgeting, managing time, presentations, assertiveness, etc.
- Things need to change but don't know how to do it or where to start.
- Productivity is low and needs to improve.
- Low morale indications: absenteeism, sickness, lateness, etc.
- Destructive relationships with other departments.
- Poor internal conflict handling.
- Low trust levels between individuals.
- Poor relationships, sniping, sarcasm, etc.
- Deadlines not being met.
- Overworked and overstressed people.
- Support for personnel decisions: selection, promotion, dismissal, etc.

Less genuine motivations

- Supporting decisions already taken.
- Doing what management are frightened to do.
- Being an extra 'pair of hands'.
- Surfacing difficulties the manager knows are there but doesn't want to admit to.
- Calling in a consultant is seen as the thing to do.
- To deputize for internal resources which are difficult to get.
- To provide objectivity to an otherwise subjective decision.
- Supporting incompetent managers by covering up their deficiencies.
- Helping to spend money left in the budget at the end of the financial year which will be lost otherwise.
- Covering up serious errors which may be discovered by audit.
- To prove that the problems belong to someone else, or that they are not the manager's fault.
- To lay the blame for the problem on another department.

Genuine motivations—contd.

- A declining marketplace or market share.
- Poor communications across, downwards and upwards.
- Constant 'firefighting', rather than solving the real problems.
- Lack of innovation: technical, product, human resource policies.
- Complacency about what the organization is doing now: 'as is' contentment.
- Strategic ambiguity—nobody really sure where the organization is headed or why.

5 Contracting

What is contracting?

All relationships between people are based on expectations in one form or another. Sometimes a few of these expectations are explicitly stated and agreed (as in marriage), more often they are assumed and taken for granted. Yet despite the absence of discussion and shared agreement, expectations still exist. If violated they may cause disruption and disagreement and in extreme cases a breakdown of the relationship. For example, a friendship may be founded on each person providing support and encouragement for the other. If circumstances arise where one person can no longer provide support, then unless a new basis is found the relationship is highly likely to deteriorate and founder. In consulting, open discussion of expectations is essential as the foundation for good contracting.

In essence, contracting is the stage in the consultation process where, together with the client, you attempt to crystallize and make explicit:

- your expectations of the relationship
- who will do what—i.e. commitment to action
- any boundaries which may exist

In this respect, contracting is about ownership. But it is not easy. Given that clients have invited you in to help overcome some difficulty or problem, you could find that they wish to move to problem solving as quickly as possible. Consequently, as with gaining entry, spending time agreeing the details of a contract may be seen as a waste of time. However, we believe it is essential to resist the pressure to move to problem solving even if this causes some anxiety. Unless you are clear where you are going at the outset, you cannot measure whether you have reached your destination. Similarly with contracting, it is essential that both you and your clients understand where you are going.

It is also important to note that, although contracting has legal overtones, it is not meant to be an instrument for either side to bludgeon the other into compliance. Contracting is simply a process where both parties can clarify what the other wants.

Who do I contract with?

In our view it is essential that contracts are agreed with all who are involved in the client system. Bearing in mind that contracting is about ownership and commitment, unless the whole client system is committed to change, it is likely to fail at some stage. This is commonly seen in training situations. Probably all trainers have had the experience of running a course where participants do not recognize they have a problem. In most instances where this occurs the agreement about the training will have been confirmed with the participant's manager. Although the manager may recognize the problem he or she will rarely have pointed this out to the staff. Instead, 'Training' will have been invited to sort out the problem by designing an appropriate course. Trainers who collude with this approach effectively allow the manager to dump the problem in their lap. Furthermore, regardless of what training methods they choose, if the staff do not accept there is a problem, the effectiveness of the training will be much reduced.

If a more effective outcome is desired, you must ensure that the contract is agreed with all elements of the client system. The scenario described in the previous paragraph is inevitably a recipe for failure.

Assignments which involve complex client systems will inevitably lead to contracts with each of the parties. It is important, therefore, to ensure that all the contracts complement each other. If at all possible you might try to encourage each of the different parties in the client system to contract with each other.

How to start contracting

As we saw from the previous chapter, meaningful contracting can only start once both you and the clients have gained sufficient entry to talk openly with one another. The key issue in this hinges on the word 'sufficient'. Unfortunately, as with many other aspects of consulting, there are no hard and fast rules. The key question that you need to bear in mind is 'Have I gained sufficient entry to move on?'. As we saw earlier, this is a matter of personal judgement. Having decided to move on, the next question is 'How?'. In many consultations the flow into contracting will occur naturally as clients start to outline what they want. You are then free to respond and bring in other agenda items as appropriate. In other instances you may initiate contracting yourself, in which case it is possible to start from a number of different angles. These could include:

1 A direct question about the reason for needing your help;
2 A direct question about why the client chose you from among other consultants who may have been available;
3 Initiating a discussion about the expected relationship between you and the client system;
4 Initiating a discussion about the relationships within the client system.

Each of these starting points will open discussion in a different area of contracting, and all can be important in different situations. For example, questions about the need for help tackle the substance of the consultation and are probably the most common starting point. Questions concerning 'why choose me?' may be vital in instances where other consultants have failed or been rejected. Questions about relationships tackle the issue of how the client expects to work with you. All are legitimate points of entry but whatever your starting point all need to be covered at some stage.

In a few cases you may find that you are well under way or have completed contracting when you start to encounter the consequences of insufficient entry (as described in the previous chapter). In such circumstances you have little option other than to abandon any progress so far and return to gaining entry.

This happened to the authors during one particular assignment. At the first meeting with the client an initial contract was apparently agreed. However, a few days later we were called to an unscheduled second meeting. At the meeting a new person was present who was not party to the initial contract agreement. During the meeting he made it obvious that he wanted several new elements added to the contract together with various other amendments. It was clear he was angry at not being involved in the earlier meeting and was deliberately creating difficulties. In response, we abandoned our attempts at contracting and instead tried to gain entry with the new client group. Eventually it emerged that the new member had been deliberately excluded from the first meeting as the others feared he would be 'difficult'. Only when these issues had been worked through were we able to return to contracting, but this time on a more meaningful basis with the whole client system. It is our hunch that had we gone ahead with the assignment on the initial contract (which, in retrospect, was made with only part of the client system) we would have encountered serious problems later—perhaps jeopardizing the whole assignment.

Having examined when and how to start contracting (and what to do if sufficient entry has not been gained), we must consider next what needs to be discussed.

Discussion points during contracting

The level of detail that you will need to discuss during contracting will vary from one assignment to the next, depending on the nature of the assignment and the potential difficulties envisaged. Yet it would appear that client and consultant expectations operate at two levels. By way of illustration, we recall a conversation with a public relations officer in a large organization during which she commented, 'You can tell who are the outsiders here almost immediately.' In making this observation she was highlighting the difference between the bulk of employees who had started with the company in their youth and worked their way up and a few others who were usually professionally qualified but had joined the organization later in their careers. When asked to explain, she pointed out that the difference lay not so much in *what* outsiders did but *how* they did it—somehow their methods of doing things and ways of working were different. For us, this illustration highlights the two levels that need to be covered in contracting. The first, or formal level, includes the more obvious expectations about *what* will be done. The second, or informal level, concerns mainly expectations and assumptions about *how* it will be done.

The concerns that need to be covered at the formal level are generally more obvious and include:

- What service or activity will you carry out?
- What is the time-scale for the assignment?
- How much will it cost the organization?

As a general rule this level of contracting is easily identified and rarely overlooked. By contrast, informal aspects of contracting are much more subtle and difficult to pin down. Over and above any agreement about the assignment itself, you and your client will have a whole host of other assumptions about the relationship. These could include:

- How you should behave
- How you should collect information
- Issues concerning confidentiality
- Level of commitment expected
- The match between your value system and that of the client
- What you mean by the words you use

It is clear that unless these informal expectations are made explicit and understood at the outset they can obstruct and eventually undermine the whole assignment. Even something as simple as inappropriate dress can put you in a situation where, whatever your expertise, you will be discounted by the client. Similarly, misunderstanding about the words and expressions we use can lead to problems. For example, managers frequently use terms like 'work hard', 'participation', 'confidential', etc., but do they mean the same as our interpretation? The only way we can be sure is to explore with clients what they really mean, in the hope of reaching a mutual understanding of the concepts and constructs we use.

Many of these kinds of assumptions are taken for granted within organizations and as a result they often do not come to light until they surface as problems during an assignment. It is useful therefore to look at potential difficulties.

Difficulties

There are many assumptions and expectations which could cause difficulty during your assignments. But, before looking at our list, stop for a few moments; use your own experience and thoughts about consulting to generate your list of potential problems.

Our response was as follows:

Previous history
- Is this the first time a consultant has been used?
- What has the client tried before?

Expectations of the consultant
- Why has the client chosen you for this assignment?
- What is your bias?
- Is an outcome expected in terms of results, changes, solutions, recommendations, savings, or a combination of these?

Time/resource allocation
- Is your time fixed or open-ended?

- What time/resources is the client expected to put in?
- How much departmental time will be needed?

Organizational relationships
- Do these enable or constrain?
- Who can you speak/not speak to?
- What can you discuss?
- What topics/information must you avoid?
- Are there any power/authority difficulties?

Methodology
- What methodology are you expected to use for data gathering:
  - action research?
  - questionnaires?
  - interviews?
  - informal discussion?
  - attitude surveys?
- Are any specific data-gathering methods excluded?

Level of commitment/involvement
- Is the client the owner of the problem? What does this mean with respect to commitment and involvement?
- What level or kind of commitment is required from the client?
- Is the client's manager or any other group/department involved?

Confidentiality
- What does confidentiality mean with respect to the problem, the data and any recommendations?
- Can data be collected/reported anonymously?
- Who can share any data gathered? The people who supplied it? The client? The client's manager?
- Will any aspect of the assignment be reported on a wider scale or published?

Termination/renegotiation
- Who can initiate renegotiation of the contract if the problem changes or if the problem is found to be outside the original agreement?
- Who can terminate the assignment?

This list is not meant to be exhaustive and inevitably you will run into difficulties which either you never envisaged at the outset or are unique to a particular organization or department. Nevertheless, it should give you a reasonable overview of the kinds of issues you should bear in mind when engaging in contracting discussions.

Having looked at the difficulties you may need to discuss, it is perhaps sensible to turn next to how you can minimize them.

Minimizing the difficulties

Given that it is highly unlikely you will be able to anticipate all difficulties beforehand, it is important to address what strategies you might employ to ensure that unexpected problems are minimized. A few suggestions follow:

- Accept from the outset that the nature of a contract is dynamic and always open to renegotiation from either side. Following from this, it is equally important that clients have a similar understanding. Should difficulties then arise there is permission for either side to request renegotiation.
- Help clients to state what they really *do* want as opposed to what they feel they *ought* to want.
- Be clear about who else will be involved, how they will be kept informed and how their inputs will be managed.
- Remain constantly aware that the problem as defined by the client may not, in the event, turn out to be the real problem. However, 'start where the client is' is usually good advice.

The optimum outcome of contracting

Ideally, the outcome of contracting is some form of agreement on what is to be undertaken, at what expense and under what terms. Although this can be simply a verbal agreement, a written contract can be very helpful in testing mutual understanding (i.e. Is what I think I said the same as what you think I said and is it what we both mean, and vice versa?). Obviously, the detail you include will vary from one assignment to the next depending on the nature of the assignment and the potential difficulties envisaged. However, as a minimum, we believe all contracts should include:

- A statement about the aims and objectives of the assignment. This should be as explicit as possible and include a statement on how you would judge success. This will then permit much easier evaluation of whether the venture has been worth while.
- An outline of the first steps. This should aim to give a clear picture of how both you and the client will proceed.
- Identification of who will be involved in the assignment and the division of responsibilities.
- Any potentially difficult area, if it appears important that this should be included: e.g. methodology, levels of involvement, confidentiality, etc.
- A statement defining the dynamic nature of the contract and giving permission for either party to request renegotiation if this becomes necessary.
- Time-scale of the assignment and the disengagement plan. It may seem somewhat surprising to raise the issue of disengagement before the assignment is really under way, but it is our experience that the best time to talk about endings is at the beginning. In a strange way it can help to reassure the client that your intentions are honest. The rationale behind this will be discussed more fully in Chapter 9 which deals with disengagement and follow-up.
- Provision of some form of review of the assignment both during it and when it is complete so that both parties have ongoing and end-point evaluation of the success or otherwise of the consultation.
- An assessment of the cost to the client. In most cases this will include

obvious costs such as your time, any additional resources that may be needed and the client's time. Equally, there may be recurrent costs to take into account such as the cost of ongoing back-up or support. Also there could be hidden costs which are very difficult to quantify; e.g. if redundancies are likely as a result of taking on a new system there will be hidden emotional costs not only for those directly involved but also those indirectly involved.

Other contracting issues are summarized in the checklists at the end of this chapter.

An exercise in contracting
Think of a relationship with a colleague at work and list on a sheet of paper:

- What you expect of the colleague
- What you think the colleague expects of you

When you are responding try to take into account the following points:

- Why you chose this particular relationship
- What you gain from the relationship
- What you would be prepared to do or not do within the relationship
- What behaviour is acceptable or unacceptable
- How you expect to manage and resolve differences
- How much time you expect to give one another
- Boundaries of confidentiality in your conversations

When you can't think of anything else, review your list and put a tick against all those items which have been explicitly discussed with your colleague. Then consider the implications of what this says about the 'taken for granted' assumptions you have made in this relationship.

An even better variation on this exercise is to invite the colleague to do the exercise as well (but obviously from his or her point of view). When you have both finished, compare and discuss your lists. You might even find it helps to develop the relationship between the two of you.

You may like to try the exercise again, this time focusing on a close personal relationship—say, a close friend or your partner or spouse.

Other outcomes of contracting

The discussion earlier looked at the optimum outcome from contracting and highlighted the areas of agreement which may be reached. Unfortunately, it is not always the case that the optimum outcome is possible. Indeed, we would suggest that if you are ever in a situation where you feel that you have covered every contractual detail with a client, then beware; in our experience organizational life is rarely so simple. Contracting is often a difficult process and may be spread over a number of meetings. Although the optimum outcome is desirable other legitimate outcomes could include:

- Agreeing the broad basis of a contract covering the main points but (where both parties feel comfortable) leaving the detail until later.

- Situations where you agree to write a tentative draft contract that will provide the basis for further discussion.
- Establishing initial contact and gaining entry but agreeing to go no further at this stage—however, the door is left open for collaboration at a later date.
- Mutual agreement not to embark on an assignment together with a clear understanding why not.

The important point which arises from this is that you must feel free not to press ahead with any assignment if important contractual details are unresolved. Having said this, we recognize that refusing to accept an assignment could have important implications for the internal consultant:

- The effect on your career
- The effect on any bonus or performance-related reward system
- The effect on your appraisal
- How will your manager react—will he or she support you?
- The effect on your department
- Will you ever be invited back by that client?
- Does the organizational culture support individuals who say no?

Clearly, when deciding whether to refuse an assignment you will need to take these factors into account. We would be the last to condemn anyone who feels obliged to accept a contract which is less than satisfactory. Indeed, in the politics of organizational life there could be perfectly valid reasons for accepting a contract where you are not completely happy. On occasions we have accepted contracts where we were less than one hundred per cent certain in order to gain entry for further work. However, these were not decisions we took in silence; our reservations were made explicit to the respective client groups. Equally, they were not decisions that were made without assessing the implications. We would argue that our rationale for such decisions is similar to that of the supermarket which offers a 'loss leader'; it may be worth it in the long run.

Consequences of poor contracting

At the risk of labouring the point we cannot emphasize too strongly the importance of full and open discussion during the contracting phase. Phillips and Shaw (1989) point out in their book, *A Consultancy Approach for Trainers*: 'Probably all consultants would agree that problems arising in later stages of an assignment can be traced back to poor initial contracting or failure to renegotiate the contract as circumstances change.'

Even when you recognize all these dangers you could still experience enormous client pressure to move quickly into problem solving once you have agreed the formal aspects of contracting. However, the following illustration gives some indication of the distasteful consequences which could result if you fail to address adequately the informal details of contracting.

The particular assignment consisted of working with a group of highly specialized IT staff. They were all technical experts in their fields but had 'topped out' in terms of their longer-term career prospects. As they all worked in some form of consulting role they were to be offered the opportunity to examine their consulting skills as part of a wider personal development programme. The assignment was offered to the authors only a few weeks before the programme began. By this stage all other details of the programme had been fixed except for a one-day slot which had been left for consulting skills. The contracting meeting was held with the training officer where he insisted it was to be left to our discretion how we wanted to work with the group. After agreeing the formal levels of the contract we attempted to explain our approach. This was to assume a high level of experience in the client group and start where they were. The training officer appeared to accept this and emphasized that he believed that we knew what we were doing and that how we ran the day was our decision. We accepted the work and sent the client a proposal describing how we would structure the day. Although this was accepted, the event proved to be a disaster. Our efforts to work with the group met with refusal and we were clearly informed by the group that the day should have consisted of expert instruction on 'how to consult' together with a few 'war stories'. In effect, our way of working was alien to both the group's expectations and the organizational culture (which revered and rewarded the expert).

In retrospect we should have picked up the cues given out at the contracting meeting and either pushed for more involvement by the client or turned down the assignment. We allowed ourselves to collude with one part of the client system, ignoring the rest. The result was a failed assignment. On a more positive note, we learned a great deal about the importance of the informal level of contracting and resolved to ensure it is never compromised in the future.

Renegotiating the contract

In the previous example there was no opportunity for us to renegotiate the contract once the assignment had started to go wrong. Thankfully, this is not always the case—with many assignments it is possible to renegotiate as the work progresses. However, you do need to plan for this from the very start.

You can prompt renegotiation as a result of a variety of issues. First, information may come to light during an assignment which changes either the nature or scope of the work. Second, situations do arise where one of the parties fails to deliver their part of the original contract. Both of these situations make renegotiation imperative. However, it is important to recognize that renegotiation is not a sign of weakness or failure on your part. It is simply being open and honest and facing up to the implications of a changing situation rather than carrying on blindly.

Perhaps the best way you can prepare for the possibility of renegotiation is by ensuring that this provision is discussed early in the contracting stage. It is then very easy for either you or your client to initiate renegotiation without loss of face.

Summary

- Contracting involves an open sharing of expectations between consultant and client.
- Contracts need to be agreed with everyone involved in the client system.
- Meaningful contracts can only be established when both client and consultant have gained sufficient entry with one another.
- Contracts need to embrace expectations at both formal and informal levels.
- Contracting may confront many difficulties.
- There can be several legitimate outcomes ranging from a satisfactory working agreement through to mutual agreement not to embark on the project.
- The consequences of poor contracting can lead to severe difficulties later.
- An option to renegotiate needs to be agreed from the start of any project.

Checklist 5.1 *The purpose of the contract*

A good contract

- Helps define the problem further;
- Clarifies in both the client's and the consultant's minds the work to be done;
- Avoids unnecessary work and work on wrong problems;
- Provides the consultant with parameters and freedom to act within them;
- Gives the client an understanding of how to work with the consultant and what to expect from him or her;
- Sets mutual expectations, goals and objectives;
- Establishes the ground rules for behaviour between the client and the consultant over such things as anonymity of data, mutual feedback, legitimacy of differences, etc.

Checklist 5.2 *Strong and weak contracts*

A strong contract is central to success. Its characteristics are:

- High commitment by all parties to make the contract
- Clear commitment in terms of time
- Clear statement of objectives
- Mutual trust and respect
- Risks and anxieties in the open

A weak contract has these characteristics:

- The consultant has uneasy feelings, and is not sure why.
- The client's extent of commitment is unclear.

- The client is under many other stresses, and so the activity has low priority.
- There is inadequate planning time before the event.
- The client abdicates all responsibility to the consultant.

Checklist 5.3   *Testing the contract*

It is time to test, and perhaps end, a contract when:

- The client keeps putting things off.
- Agreements are made, and forgotten (by either side).
- The consultant has a higher personal commitment to the outcome than the client.
- The client looks to the consultant to do things he or she should be doing.
- The client is doing well, and does not really need any more help.

Checklist 5.4   *Contracting—general issues*

A contract is a way of making expectations explicit, trying to anticipate misunderstandings and setting out each side of the bargain, as it were. A contract need not be in writing but there are certain aspects of your work together which need to be discussed before you start. The following is a list which seems to cover most of the essential aspects. No doubt you can add to it.

Hierarchical relationships
- are we constrained by them?
- what can I say and to whom?
- what power/authority problems?

How much time allocation?
- consultant's time/open-ended?
- client's time?
- departmental time, etc.?

How much freedom do we have?
- consultant?
- client?

What commitment is there?
- from my boss?
- client's boss?
- owners of the problem?

What are the expectations?
- of consultant?
- of client?
- of consultant's boss?
  in terms of: results
               changes
               solutions
               recommendations
               savings

What methods can I use?
- data gathering?
- action research?

	• questionnaires?
	• interviews?
	• attitude surveys?
	• what modes are barred to me?
Who can share the data?	• people who supplied it?
	• client?
	• client's boss?
	• my boss?
To whom do I report?	• who owns the report?
	• client's boss?
	• client?
Who can end the consultation?	• client or client's boss?
	• consultant or consultant's boss?
The issue of confidentiality	• of the problem
	• of the data
	• of the recommendations, etc.
	• can data be anonymous?
Renegotiation	• who can do it?
	• if the problem changes
	• if the project extends outside the department
Starting the consultation	• where, when, how?
	• we may not be able to say where we are going but we can say where we start from
What has gone before?	• is this the first time?
	• what has the client tried already?
To whom am I responsible?	• client?
	• client's boss?
	• my boss?
Cost	• who pays?
	• whose budget?
	• who can authorize more resources in time, money, materials?

6 Collecting data

What is data?

Once you have a contract the next step is to gather data that will help you and the client clarify the nature of the problem, isolate symptoms, identify causes and lead towards some kind of resolution of the problem. The dilemma, of course, is what kind of data you should collect. What data is likely to be relevant and what irrelevant?

To some extent data collection will depend on the technical discipline of the consultant. The accountant will collect financial and control data; the personnel manager is likely to see the client's problem in terms of payment systems, recruitment or industrial relations; the marketing consultant is likely to be interested in the product or service itself and the marketplace in which it is being sold.

We believe, however, that if you remain too firmly rooted in your basic technical discipline then you are likely to disregard important elements of the organizational problem. A good consultant is a bit like a detective in an Agatha Christie novel. The reader is presented with all kinds of evidence, much of which is dismissed as irrelevant. Hercule Poirot or Miss Marple, on the other hand, are able to recognize the significance of seemingly unrelated and irrelevant events, which when put together reveal the identity of the murderer.

The consultant too is often presented with an array of complex information about the client department, the systems, the technology, the structures and the people. Faced with this complexity it is very tempting to focus on that part of the client system that is made easy to understand by one's technical discipline. However, most organizational problems cross functional boundaries. If, for example, a major new system is being introduced there may well be recruitment, training and financial implications. If a new product is being developed there are likely to be technical, financial, systems and human dimensions to the change. Consultants helping with such changes can't afford to remain too firmly rooted in their basic discipline. If you are to be successful as a consultant it is important that you are able to make connections between often disparate pieces of information and put them together so that they make sense and produce the big picture. This way you can help the client to deal with the complete problem instead of tinkering with part of it.

There is one kind of data which is always available but all too often neglected. This is data about the human dimension of the problem. Your *raison d'être* as a consultant is organizational change and such change affects and is affected by people. Many consultants are aware that the managerial style and morale in the client department have a huge impact on the success of the department and on the outcome of the project they are working on. But they feel that they have been asked to explore a 'business problem' and don't want to 'get involved with personalities'. If you do this then you ignore a lot of data which impacts significantly on the business issue. A fall in sales may well have something to do with pricing, quality, advertising or promotional activities. But equally it may be affected by the style of the sales manager; the morale, motivation and commitment of salespeople; political in-fighting between sales managers; an unwillingness to communicate openly with other departments; or a feeling among salespeople of being unsupported. A technical innovation might be less successful if the people involved feel threatened by the change; if they feel that their views haven't been taken into account; that their skills have been devalued or that they themselves are not valued by 'the management'.

This exotic data is very difficult to collect and quantify, and can be ambiguous. However, you ignore it at your peril (Checklist 6.1 at the end of the chapter summarizes questions to help gather this type of data). Ultimately, the success of a consulting project will depend not only on how you handle the purely business problem but also on how comfortable you are dealing with the data you collect about the human beings who will be affected and their relationships with each other. These types of issues are illustrated in the following example.

Some time ago one of the authors was hired to carry out some sales training in the publishing industry. The client company printed newspapers and periodicals. It appeared to be a fairly straightforward assignment. The sales representatives had hitherto been in a distribution role, liaising with wholesalers, retailers and their own head office to ensure that the products passed through the distribution chain efficiently and arrived at the retail outlets in time. Obviously, this is crucially important in an industry where the product has an extremely short shelf life. Henceforth, following a number of structural changes in the company, the role of the representatives was to change and they were being given more responsibility for increasing circulation of the products in their area. This meant they would have to call on retailers to persuade them to give more prominence to the products. To do this they needed training in basic selling skills. When the author arrived to work with the first group, however, there was an atmosphere of anger and resentment. They did not know why they were there, or why they needed these skills. They did not understand the changes that had been made and resented them. Needless to say, they responded very negatively to the training session.

What the author had done, of course, was to ignore some very important data. His first meeting with the national sales manager at head office had been constantly interrupted by telephone calls and people 'putting their heads round the door' seeking urgent information or decisions. The environment seemed to be seething with high activity and urgency, minute-to-minute changes and consequent decisions to be made. It was exciting but it was also frenetic. Subsequent meetings with field sales managers revealed a picture of a group of very able and dynamic people, with lots of energy, but all doing very stressful jobs. What the author did not realize then was that they were spending most of the day at home chained to the telephone in constant contact with various headquarters people. This left them very little time to spend with the representatives. Consequently, the representatives were facing a very uncertain future, they had had very little individual communication about the organizational changes and, inevitably, there were lots of rumours about further changes, cut-backs and redundancies. They had little opportunity to talk through their changing role with their managers and they looked unlikely to get much personal support as they adapted to the new role. Little wonder they reacted as they did. The author eventually decided it was pointless to carry on with the sales training sessions without helping all the clients to examine more fundamental problems of communication, decision making and management style within the department.

Categorizing data

Having recognized the range and complexity of the data available to consultants no doubt you will need a vehicle to help make sense of it all. This should help you categorize the data so that it becomes manageable and usable. You will then be in a position to feed it back to clients in the form of information that helps them understand the situation more clearly and make informed decisions about the way forward.

To do this you need some models of organizations and organizational behaviour in your own work. We have found two models very helpful in making sense of the data collected during a variety of assignments.

Organization diagnostic model

The first of these models divides organizational activities into a number of interdependent spheres. These spheres are all crucial to organizational success and all need to be given managerial attention (see Figure 6.1).

When diagnosing organizational problems you need to be sensitive to all six of these spheres. The symptoms of a problem might emerge in one sphere but some of the causes might lie in others. For example, a construction company identified that it had a problem in the Task sphere; sales volume was not increasing as it should. The sales force was divided into geographical areas while most of their customers tended to have national operations which meant that orders taken by one sales force might result in work actually being done in a different area. The area sales teams seemed very reluctant to cooperate with each other when dealing with these large national customers. Communication between areas was minimal and no effort was made to keep each other informed or support each other. The problem was diagnosed as a People issue and a lot of energy was put into communication and teamworking events. This had some effect but the problems of poor communication

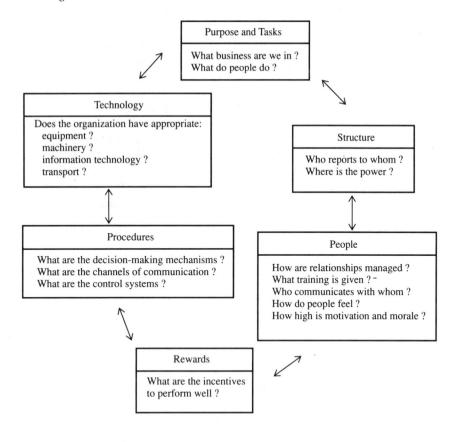

Figure 6.1 *Organization diagnostic model*

and cooperation persisted. What no one had recognized was that at least part of the equation lay in the sphere of Rewards. The area sales teams were given a group bonus which relied not only on sales volume achieved but also on being more successful than the other teams. The management wanted people to cooperate but they were actually being rewarded to compete with each other. A broader diagnosis would have resulted in an earlier resolution of the problem.

The quest for total quality management (TQM) is also a good illustration of an organizational change strategy which can go badly wrong if attention is not given to all six spheres of activity. The authors became involved with a TQM programme which seemed to be running out of steam. The top team had done a lot of work producing a mission statement (Purpose and Tasks). Each department had a clear and agreed departmental purpose analysis (Structure) which clarified the expectations not only of the manager but of each department's internal suppliers and internal or external customers. A lot of work was done on clarifying quality standards (Procedures) and systems for ensuring they were met. In addition, quality groups were set up as a way of encouraging employees to develop ideas for solving problems. Finally, it was obvious that the technology was adequate for the needs of the business. So what was going wrong?

It became evident that the bits of jigsaw that were missing were in the spheres of Rewards and People. The company still used a piece-work system so that people were being rewarded for quantity of work not for quality. They were really being rewarded for conforming rather than for taking responsibility for quality or suggesting innovation. This linked of course with the sphere of People and how they were managed. The senior team now began to recognize that TQM requires the company to work towards having 'TQM people', who feel empowered and valued rather than controlled and mistrusted. The senior team did some work on identifying the kind of people they needed if they were to have a truly TQM business. This led them to think through the implications for management style. They realized that if they wanted employees to work in a TQM way they could no longer use a management style based on coercion, mistrust, closed communication channels, and an emphasis on punishment rather than on rewards—especially psychological rewards. They began to recognize that what they had done so far was important, but to achieve genuine TQM they needed to embark on a very ambitious programme of cultural and personal change if they were to be really successful.

Group working model

A second approach to categorizing the data available during the diagnostic phase of the consultation is to divide it into three categories:

- the task
- the systems and procedures
- the process

Whenever two or more people work together on any kind of enterprise there are three different strands of activity in getting from point A, the start, to point B, the finish. These three strands are always present regardless of the number of people, the length of time the organization has existed, the time available or the complexity of the task. The model applies equally whether examining a group of people who have come together to achieve a single simple objective or an organization of thousands of people which has complex objectives and a long history.

The task

This is a statement of what has to be achieved: the content of the work. It is data concerning the conversion of information, opinions and ideas of group members into decisions or recommendations, or the conversion of raw materials into manufactured articles. In general it concerns *what* has to be done and *why*. It is important that all members of a team,

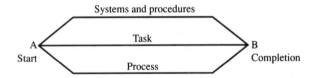

Figure 6.2   Group working model

department or organization have a clear understanding of exactly what the task is. Often the task is left unstated with everyone assuming they have the same perception of what is to be achieved, while in fact people are working towards slightly different objectives with differing priorities. The result is organizational chaos. It is important for an organization to have a clear mission statement. People in the organization need to know what business they are in, what goals are to be achieved and how success will be measured. When agreeing the task it is important to ensure that it is realistic and that sufficient resources are available in the form of money, equipment, people and time.

The systems and procedures
This covers *how* the people in the team need to organize themselves in order to get the work done and achieve the task. It addresses such questions as:

- How do we acquire additional resources?
- Who does what?
- Who fills the necessary roles?
- How will we keep to time?
- How will we monitor progress?
- How will we review what we have done?
- How do we make changes to the schedule?

The systems and procedures are the mechanics of organizational life. Such activities will include:

- planning procedures
- programming and scheduling systems, e.g. critical path analysis
- budgetary controls
- financial and systems audit
- business systems
- organization structures
- roles and job descriptions
- controls and guidelines
- company policies
- procedures and processes for making decisions, ensuring people's contribution, etc.
- reward systems
- discipline systems
- quality control
- reporting systems
- contract procedures
- purchasing procedures

The process
If the systems and procedures are the mechanical aspects of getting things done, then the process is the organic part of organizational life. The task and the systems and procedures don't take account of human beings with their hopes, fears, aspirations and feelings. Process is the part of the model which takes these into account. Process data is about the interactions that take place between members of the group or with other people in the immediate environment. It is about how people

work together, their relationships and the feelings engendered by their behaviour.

Process issues in teams or organizations would include:

- management style
- who makes decisions and how
- communications: one-way or two-way
- who participates in decision making
- status
- perceived power or powerlessness
- do people feel listened to?
- how people react to new ideas—constructively or destructively?
- opportunities for individual development and growth
- the degree of support, openness and trust
- the amount of feedback people give to each other
- how conflict is handled—constructively or destructively?
- do people compete with each other or work collaboratively?
- how problems about gender, race and disability are handled
- the way feelings are handled
- involvement
- commitment
- motivation

It will be obvious that a client group which concentrates solely on its *systems and procedures* and its *process* may have a wonderful time but is unlikely to achieve the *task*. It will not be long before morale will suffer and the group disintegrates or is disbanded. However, concentration solely upon the task is likely to lead to other problems. Arguments will probably develop about 'who does what', questions will be posed about objectives and bad feelings will probably be the order of the day.

Although the symptoms of neglect of everything but the task are obvious to all, few groups choose to discuss them openly. Such discussion is often regarded as a waste of time and, as a consequence, interpersonal issues tend to be ignored, only to reappear later as 'corridor comments'. It is a sign of group maturity when issues are openly expressed and dealt with; when group building is regarded as an integral part of achieving the task.

Most consultants are invited to deal with problems that look like task or systems and procedures issues: problems to do with scheduling work, controlling how work is done, reorganizing the structure, etc. However, whatever the presenting problem, there will inevitably be a human, process dimension which will be much more ambiguous and difficult to handle. Unless you collect process data, present it to the client and help the client to deal with it, your impact and influence will be diminished. If you fail to take account of process data you will be unlikely to be able to assess the impact of the problem on the whole organization.

Of course, persuading people to examine and discuss process issues can be very difficult. People can be very reluctant to work on the process problems that affect a working group.

Exercise

Why do you think people might be reluctant to identify and work on process problems? Write down as many reasons as you can and then compare them with our list at the end of the chapter (see Exercise 1).

One final word of caution. When deciding what data to collect it is important to examine your own motives for collecting it. It could be tempting to collect data to support a pet theory, to prove how unpopular and incompetent a manager is, or how clever you are. If you do this you are collecting data for your own benefit. The client-centred consultant only collects data for the benefit of the client.

It is also important that you fully discuss the boundaries of data collection with clients at the contracting stage. As early as possible you should try to raise clients' awareness that there may be a human dimension to the project. Try to get agreement to collect process data as well as systems and procedures and task data. Reassure clients about confidentiality but make sure they are prepared for the possibility that some of the data may make them feel a little uncomfortable.

Having identified what data to collect we now need to turn our attention to the problems of how to carry out data collection.

Data collection

There is a limited number of ways of collecting data from your client system and they all have potential advantages and disadvantages. The methods are:

- interviews
- questionnaires
- direct observation
- document analysis
- your own experience and intuition

Interviews

You can conduct interviews with individuals or with groups. The interview can be open-ended and unstructured or it can be carried out in a more structured way.

Advantages

- The data is very rich. You can pick up a lot of information from the way questions are answered, non-verbal signals, what is not said, etc.
- Sometimes issues emerge during data-collection interviews which could not have been predicted.
- Interviewing people can help you to build relationships, and gain a deeper entry with people in the client system.

Disadvantages

- The cost—interviews can be very expensive and time-consuming.
- Only a restricted number of people can be interviewed.
- It can be difficult to interpret the data.
- Interviewer bias.
- It can be difficult to quantify the data.
- Data can be subjective.
- Data may not be comparable unless interviews are tightly structured.

Questionnaires   A lot of information can be obtained by the use of surveys and questionnaires.

Advantages   • Useful with large numbers of people.
• It is relatively inexpensive.
• People may be more honest if the questionnaire is completed anonymously.
• It can be easier to quantify the data.

Disadvantages   • Predetermined questions can miss important issues.
• People might be suspicious of an impersonal questionnaire. There is no opportunity to give reassurances, to explain the purpose of collecting the data or to point out the potential benefits to the
• respondent.
• It is possible to over-interpret the results of questionnaires and read too much into them.

Direct observation   If you go out into your client group and watch them at work you can build up a very clear understanding of the way they work now. Sometimes you may be able to observe while they try things differently. This is often the role of the sports coach—acting as informed, critical observer feeding back to the athletes information about their strengths and weaknesses. You may not be an athletics coach but you may well decide to sit in at meetings of your client group, make calls with the salespeople, spend time on the factory floor, look at the technology or experience the working conditions.

Sometimes you will observe and give immediate feedback to the client. At other times you may need to keep a more permanent record of what you have seen in the form of notes. You may also use a camera or a video or tape recorder to gather directly audible or visible data.

Advantages   • You can observe the way people actually behave rather than the way they say they behave.
• You can collect data about what is happening now rather than what has happened in the past.
• Often the outsider can see things that group members are unaware of.
• Issues that could not have been predicted might become obvious during the observation.

Disadvantages   • Direct observation can be time-consuming and expensive.
• The data might be narrow and selective.
• You can only observe what happens while you are present. You might miss significant issues or events.
• Your presence might affect the way people behave.
• Observer bias—if you see someone you like you might assume that what that person does is good.
• Sometimes people's perceptions of events are different from the reality.

Document analysis A method much used by consultants is to spend time looking at the numbers, the balance sheet, the statistics and written communication. This method can give you a lot of information on things like scrap rates, rejects, absenteeism, lateness, sickness, sales, production, costs, etc.

Advantages
- It doesn't involve the client's time.
- It is inexpensive.
- It can be objective data which has a high degree of credibility with the client.

Disadvantages
- Data gathered by this method is limited to the task, and systems and procedures. It is unlikely to reveal any information on the process issues which are contributing to the problem.
- This method will tell you *what* is happening but not *why* it is happening.
- You can be tempted to hide behind the documents. This can create the illusion of being busy while avoiding the much more difficult activities of actually meeting people and asking questions.

Experience and intuition You can collect a lot of useful data about what it is like to work in the department simply by tuning in to your own feelings. The way people manage their relationships with you might be indicative of the way they manage their relationships with each other. Particularly important is your relationship with the manager. The way you are 'managed' can reveal a lot about the manager's management style. Does the manager appear open? How much freedom are you given to talk to people? How often are you expected to check back? Do you feel listened to? All this can be important data about how that manager operates. Similarly, when you are working in the department, how comfortable do you feel? Your own tensions and discomforts might be telling you something about how your clients are feeling. An illustration of this is given in the following example.

We were once asked to do some training on customer relations with a public bus company in a large provincial city. The client was astounded when we suggested that it might be a good idea for us to travel on some of the company's buses to feel what it was like to be a passenger. On entering the first bus we were greeted with an array of commands in the form of a number of notices.

- Don't talk to the driver.
- Don't stand forward of this point.
- Lower your head when leaving your seat.
- Your ticket must be retained for inspection.
- People travelling without a ticket are liable to prosecution (which someone had changed to 'persecution').
- No smoking.
- No standing on the upper deck.
- Enter only by the front door.
- Exit only by the rear door.
- Luggage must not be left in the gangway.

Of course, a good case can be made for the necessity of all these requirements. But what overall message is given to the passenger? We certainly began to feel patronized, distrusted and controlled; the general impression given was that the company would run much more smoothly if it weren't for the passengers, who made life difficult.

Using this data gathered from our own experience we were able to help the client redefine the problem which he had previously seen in narrow terms as 'How to train the bus crews in customer contact skills'. Together we redefined the problem as 'How to present a more friendly, comfortable and welcoming image to our passengers'. This changed the whole nature of the subsequent project in which customer contact training, although significant, became one part of a larger problem.

However, perhaps we should return to the advantages and disadvantages of experience and intuition.

Advantages
- The data is very solid. You know what your feelings are and no one can argue with them.
- It helps you identify sensitive issues which are difficult to observe and which people are reluctant to talk about.
- The data is immediate and about the here and now.
- You don't need permission to collect it.
- It may help you to question and challenge other data which contradicts your own experience.
- You can start collecting this kind of data as soon as you make contact with the client.

Disadvantages
- It is very subjective.
- It is open to consultant bias.
- It can be difficult to feed this data back to clients in a way that doesn't make them feel defensive.
- It can be difficult to justify.
- Some people are not very intuitive themselves and are likely to discount this kind of data.
- It can be difficult to trust your own intuition.
- It can contradict other concrete data.

Exercise
Try making a list of the kinds of questions you might ask yourself to draw on intuitive data. When you have finished, compare it with our list at the end of the chapter (see Exercise 2).

Questioning techniques

Whatever data-collection method or methods you choose you are inevitably going to need to ask questions. You may write these down in the form of surveys or questionnaires, ask them formally as part of a structured interview or very informally as you work with your clients. Asking questions is the single most important tool in the consultant's kitbag. Asking the right questions may appear very easy and yet in practice is often very difficult.

So, what are the right questions? The only answer is—it depends on your objective. However, there is one very important thing we can say about asking questions right from the start. Client-centred consultants try very hard to ask client-centred questions. What is a client-centred question, and how does it differ from those traditionally asked by consultants?

Consultants traditionally ask questions which help them understand the problem so that they can take the problem away from their clients and prescribe a solution with minimum involvement of the clients. If you are simply asking questions about information the clients already know you are probably working in a consultant-centred way.

If you are working in a client-centred way you start with the assumption that you are there to help your clients work on the problem and identify an appropriate course of action. This means asking questions which illuminate the problem for the clients, not just for the consultant. They should be questions that challenge your clients and help them think about the problem differently. Your questions should empower the clients, not diminish them. Questions also relate directly to intervention style, so you will find that many of the questions in this section have been mentioned in Chapter 2 in the context of the different intervention styles.

It is important to look at the types of questions that can be asked, what results they are likely to produce and when they are helpful or unhelpful.

Open-ended questions

Open-ended questions can be used to elicit general information. They will help you gather facts or explore your clients' feelings, opinions and attitudes. They give clients the opportunity to reply as fully as they wish, using their own words to express their thoughts and feelings. Open-ended questions invariably begin with the words 'how', 'what', 'why', 'when', 'where' or 'who'—although 'Tell me all about . . .' can also produce the same effect.

- 'What do you think has contributed to this situation?'
- 'How did you set about dealing with Mrs Smith's complaint yesterday?'
- 'Why do you do it that way?'
- 'Which part of your job do you enjoy most?'
- 'How does it feel to work around here?'
- 'What options do you have?'

These types of questions infer a non-judgemental, unbiased approach—an attitude of 'wanting to know' rather than 'telling'. Good open questions help clients to explore the situation, think the problem through in new ways and work out ways of moving forward.

Supplementary questions

Supplementary questions can be used to pursue in greater detail some information given in response to an open-ended question. This gives the client an opportunity for deeper explanation, helps to sharpen the focus without losing the natural flow. Such questions usually work best if they are not too obviously probing. Too many at one time can make clients feel pressurized or as if they are being interrogated, but they are essential for getting from the general to the real heart of the matter.

Supplementary questions are often of the 'how', 'what', 'why' type but usually linked back to what the client has just said. You might explore more deeply by asking:

- 'So when you say you were stimulated by that task, what was it that stimulated you?'
- 'So what did you feel like at that point?'
- 'That sounds interesting—could you tell me some more about that part of the job?'
- So what exactly did the customer say when you suggested that policy?'

Clarifying questions

Often you may need to check your interpretation of the information you are being given. By doing this you can ensure that you have listened and understood what has been said. You might clarify by asking questions like these:

- 'So am I right in thinking that you feel okay with the new system but feel anxious about how it will be received by the staff?'
- 'Are you saying then that it is not the extra work that you're complaining about but the fact that you feel unappreciated?'

Asking for clarification and checking your understanding of what clients have said not only builds up a clearer picture in your mind but can also help clients to crystallize what they actually feel. In the example given above the client may never have mentioned feeling unappreciated, and may not have even been conscious of it until the consultant started using checking and clarifying questions. But be wary of putting words in the client's mouth.

Reflecting

Reflecting is not strictly speaking a form of questioning but it can be a very powerful way of clarifying the importance of the words a client uses. If you listen very actively to what the client is saying he or she may use words that are more significant than they first appear. This is particularly true when 'feeling' words are used. It is often enough simply to pick up the word or phrase and reflect it back to the client.

For example, the client might say, 'I really feel like the meat in the sandwich'. On hearing this the consultant might simply reflect, 'Meat in the sandwich'.

Or the client might say, 'I really feel guilty' and the consultant might reflect: 'Guilty'.

This gives the client an opportunity to explore the significance of the word or phrase, to explore more deeply, perhaps, the stresses of feeling pressure from two directions and the causes of it. On the other hand, the client might recognize that that word or phrase doesn't really describe the situation and can now try to describe it differently. Both reactions are helpful and legitimate.

Whereas questions are always framed and therefore controlled by the consultant, by using reflecting techniques and using only the client's own words you can keep the control firmly in the hands of the client, who alone decides on the significance of the words you reflect back.

Asking about feelings

Remember to ask questions that will help both you and your clients build up a picture not only of the procedures and task aspects of the problem but also of the process dimensions of the problem. Don't be afraid to explore client feelings. People's feelings are important data. Clients won't readily tell you what they are feeling—you will only find out by asking.

You may need to be persistent. Quite often when people are asked about their feelings they actually tell you about their thoughts. For example:

Consultant 'The team seems to have made a decision which is contrary to the opinion you were putting forward. How does that feel?'

Client 'I still don't think it will work.'

Here the client has answered a 'feelings' question with a statement about his or her own thoughts rather than feelings. The consultant might need to persevere to allow clients to reveal their feelings. You might say something like:

Consultant 'You still don't agree. How does it feel working in this group?'

Client 'I feel railroaded and not listened to. I feel a bit demotivated and uncommitted to the decision.'

This time the consultant has brought to the surface some of the feelings of the team member in a way that gives the speaker and the rest of the team an opportunity to deal with the problem.

Forecasting or 'fantasy' questions

Sometimes, when working on a change programme, you may need to help clients plan for change. This can involve getting them to imagine how the change will affect them, what they will need to do differently, how they will react to the change and how they will feel about it. The purpose of forecasting or fantasy questions is to help clients explore what 'might be' or a variety of possibilities. For example:

• 'What would have to happen to show you that the organization really valued you?'
• 'Describe the perfect senior management team.'

These questions are only useful if realistic and answerable. They must be used in context, so that clients understand why such questions are being asked. However, be aware of the difficulty of interpreting the response and remember that the more 'fantastic' the question, the more difficult it is to get anything meaningful from the answer.

Less helpful questions

There are also some types of questions asked of clients which are seldom really profitable and can cause confusion or frustration. They include the five types discussed below.

Leading questions

In these, the answers are implicit in the question, in other words you almost tell the interviewees what you want their answer to be. For example: 'You find stock-taking difficult, don't you?' or 'Don't you agree that you all need more training?'.

Multiple choice questions

There is another form of leading question, but in this case the client is presented with two or more answers and asked to choose between them; e.g. 'Do you think we should send John on a course, give him an attachment or give him a book to read?'. The client may have ideas on another alternative but asking this type of question will limit the choice to the ideas presented. Equally, it restricts the answer to *one* of the alternatives whereas the client might wish to use something from all three.

Embroidered questions

This is a common questioning fault, often brought about by nervousness. In this instance the consultant asks a string of questions instead of one, either by constantly amending the phrasing or adding to the question. For example: 'What do you think about him? . . . Do you think he can do it? . . . I mean, is he all right?' This confuses clients, as they no longer know which question to answer.

Unanswerable questions

These are usually questions where clients are asked to comment on things beyond their knowledge or experience or which ask for interpretations. For example: 'What do you think made Jane do that?' In this case, Jane is the person to ask.

Statements posing as questions

These do not actually need a response and may make clients feel uncomfortable, because they are uncertain whether you wish them to comment or not. Examples are: 'Don't you think that it would be a good idea to . . . ?'; 'Don't you believe that it is best to . . . ?'

Feedback to the client

Having collected your data from the client system you now need to feed it back to your clients. Providing feedback is a crucial phase in the consulting process. Too often it is at the feedback phase that consulting assignments grind to a halt. The consultant does the research, writes a report and it gets ignored. No action is taken. If, on the other hand, you handle the feedback meeting well, your clients should have an enhanced picture of the problem but they should also have started to explore possible courses of action and be well placed to start making decisions.

Before we explore the issues involved in giving feedback, we would like to clarify what we mean by feedback. Essentially, feedback is a mechanism to enable human beings to develop, improve and change. We all need information about how we are performing whatever activity we are carrying out. We need to know how successful or effective we have been. Sometimes it is easy to get that information for ourselves. Someone learning to use a rifle will shoot at a target and get immediate feedback from the locations of the holes made in the target. That information can then be used as a basis to change and improve. Without that feedback it would be impossible to learn. Sometimes it is not possible to get this information directly; we need another person to give us feedback. This is the function of the sports coach, or the film director; their job is to feed back to the sports people or actors information about their performance that they can't acquire for themselves so that they can use the information as a basis for making improvements.

This is also your role as a consultant: to observe the client group from the outside, examine the way it operates, identify where it is effective and ineffective and feed the information back to the clients in a way that helps them understand what they are doing and make decisions about appropriate change.

One myth we often encounter is that feedback is always negative, that it is always a description of a client's inadequacies and failures. We believe that in client-centred consulting it is as important to feed back successes as it is failures. Positive feedback is as important as negative.

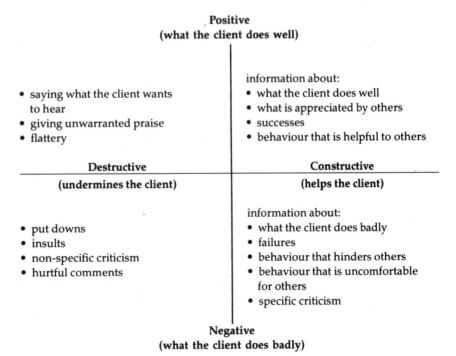

Positive
(what the client does well)

• saying what the client wants
  to hear
• giving unwarranted praise
• flattery

information about:
• what the client does well
• what is appreciated by others
• successes
• behaviour that is helpful to others

Destructive   **Constructive**
(undermines the client)   **(helps the client)**

• put downs
• insults
• non-specific criticism
• hurtful comments

information about:
• what the client does badly
• failures
• behaviour that hinders others
• behaviour that is uncomfortable
  for others
• specific criticism

Negative
(what the client does badly)

Figure 6.3 Giving feedback

What is important is that feedback should always be constructive rather than destructive. Constructive feedback, positive or negative, is designed to help the client learn, while destructive feedback simply undermines and devalues the client.

These two dimensions (positive and negative; constructive and destructive) can be illustrated diagrammatically, as shown in Figure 6.3.

Contracting and feedback

Feedback is usually about making sense of the data and links back to Chapter 5 on contracting. We believe it is important to raise the issue of feedback as early as possible. Both you and your client need to be clear at the contracting phase how feedback will be handled. You need to agree who will be given the feedback report: will circulation be restricted or will everyone who participated in interviews have access to the data that came out of the interviews? You will need to clarify what information will be confidential and what will be in the report. This is also the time when you should discuss with the client the degree to which you will feed back process as well as systems and procedures information. Don't forget that personal feedback, particularly if it is negative, can be uncomfortable to the recipient. If you feel there is a possibility that the feedback data may be confrontational then it is only fair to prepare your client at the outset. Point out this possibility when you contract so that it doesn't come as a complete surprise when you move into the feedback phase.

Timing

The best time to receive feedback, for both individuals and groups, is as close as possible to the event. It is usually a mistake to keep the data you collect to yourself until you make your final presentation. Remember your role is to facilitate change, not to produce reports. Try to feed back the data as it is collected. This will give your clients an opportunity to think about it, discuss it and make changes. Circulate an early draft of your report to everyone concerned. This gives them an opportunity to make comments and have an input into the final version and so build their own degree of commitment. By feeding information back into the client group throughout the data gathering you also facilitate a more gradual change. This can be much more comfortable for clients than asking them to implement the results of a large report which they feel has been sprung on them.

The report

What should be included in the report? Invariably, a lot more data will be collected than could ever be used and it is tempting to flood the clients with far more than they could handle. You may need to focus on three or four high-priority issues that come out of your research rather than include absolutely everything. Don't be afraid to use your intuition when deciding what to include and what to exclude. Use only enough material to give a clear picture of the situation.

It is important to keep your report as simple as possible; avoid using complicated models. Use your client's words whenever possible to cover the main points rather than technical or professional jargon. Finally, you will increase the acceptability of your ideas if you include positive data which acknowledges the successes and strengths of your clients while at the same time not shrinking from the inclusion of data which may be uncomfortable for them to face.

The feedback meeting

No doubt we have all fallen into the trap of researching a project, writing up our findings, making our recommendations and proudly handing the completed report to a senior manager who we assume will implement our recommendations. This is based on the myth that the more senior a person is in the organization, the greater his or her power to make things happen. This myth goes on to assert that mere internal consultants are powerless by comparison. However, organizational problems (especially ones which have a lot of process implications) are rarely amenable to an edict from on high. If they are to be solved they need to be discussed by everyone involved in and affected by the problem. If change is to be sustained, at some point a meeting must be called so that everyone concerned can discuss the findings of the report.

The best person to arrange the meeting is usually the person who carried out the project. If you have done the research and written the report you will be intimately involved with the problem. You know where the blockages are, and who needs to talk to whom. To be successful you may need to invite people from different departments or functions, across geographical boundaries and from a variety of tiers in the organizational hierarchy. You need to remember the definition of a client system introduced in Chapter 1—'Who knows, Who cares, Who can'. Make sure you have all three at the feedback meeting.

Your role at the feedback meeting is to help your clients clarify their understanding of the nature of the problem, help them understand each other's point of view, and encourage them to make collective decisions to which they are all committed. It is not a highly polished presentation of your findings and recommendations. Such presentations serve merely to take ownership away from your clients, inhibit discussion and put them in the role of audience rather than decision-making group. Remember that if your clients are to own the data and recommendations they need to feel that they have an opportunity to change them. So it is far better to send everyone a copy of the report in advance so they can read it and at the meeting limit yourself to a simple summary of the main findings of the report. Your role then is to facilitate the ensuing discussion.

There is likely to be some tension and resistance at the feedback meeting. A certain amount of tension is very positive—it means that people are concerned about the problem. However, be cautious if your clients simply glance casually at the data and ask 'Okay, what do we do next?' Such indifference may suggest a lack of commitment or it may indicate a reluctance to discuss the data. Apparent indifference is often a signal of resistance. On the other hand, the clients may appear very hostile, behaving aggressively towards you and your report. Whatever form resistance takes, it needs to be explored. There are often emotional reasons for resistance: people feel threatened, or exposed. They may feel they are being blamed for the problem. They may be fearful of the change that will ensue from the project. Resistance is also likely to increase the further you move away from the technical aspects of the problem and into the human dimension. The group is likely to be comfortable discussing the systems, procedures and technicalities but very uncomfortable talking about how they manage their own relationships with each other and how this impacts on the problem.

During the meeting it is important to help the group discuss any issues contained in your findings. Ask them whether the data makes sense, how the problem looks from their various perspectives, what attempts have already been made to overcome the problem. Don't try to defend the data; if people want to reject it, ask them to supply alternative data from their own experience. It is important to help the clients explore the process issues in a very supportive way. Make sure that you don't try to allocate blame or take sides. Encourage them to explore their perception of the problem in a collaborative way without trying to blame each other. Your role is to help increase mutual understanding and help them build more open relationships. You will need to use a style of working which supports and does not judge them in any way. However, this doesn't mean you should collude with the group if they attempt to deny their process and relationship problems. It is important to confront them, remembering that confrontation and support are not mutually exclusive. There may well be 'here and now' data that you can pick up at the meeting which will support your confrontation. For example, if part of the problem is an autocratic leadership style, you might point out that most of the air-time at the meeting is being taken up by the boss; or that no one seems willing to disagree with the boss; or that two people, central to the problem, don't seem to be listening to each other. Highlighting this type of immediate, 'here and now' data to supplement or enrich your confrontation can be very powerful.

As we have said before, the purpose of the feedback meeting is to help your clients to make decisions to which they are all committed. (A summary to help manage feedback meetings is given in Checklist 6.2 at the end of the chapter.) The next two chapters are devoted entirely to these important activities. In them we will describe a number of decision-making models which can be helpful and also a number of tools, ideas and pitfalls associated with building commitment.

Handling personal feedback

For many years now, whenever we have run people skills programmes (for a wide range of people including managers, internal consultants, salespeople, technicians and clerical staff, in many organizations), we have always tried to build in a session during which everyone is given an opportunity to receive feedback on how their colleagues on the programme perceive them. They hear what others see as their strengths as well as their weaknesses. They find out how people they have worked with actually feel about them and their behaviour. Almost without exception, participants find this a profound and rewarding experience.

They are invariably surprised by the amount of positive feedback they receive. They say that this feedback, positive and negative, is invaluable in helping them work on strategies for changing their behaviour back at work. What we find sad is that they also say that this is the first time anyone has given them this kind of feedback. Based on this we conclude that people in organizations very rarely share personal information with each other.

A lot of people in organizations are much less effective than they might be simply because some aspect of their behaviour is inappropriate. They may talk too much, constantly put themselves down, trivialize what they are doing with inappropriate humour, or behave in a way which others find threatening and label aggressive. The manager who is perceived as being aggressive, all things being equal, is likely to be less effective than someone who is seen to be assertive. Yet people are often unaware of the way their behaviour impacts on others. This is because, generally, people are inhibited about giving each other feedback on their behaviour and the impact it has on others. The more senior the manager the more difficult it is to get feedback. This is not only true of negative feedback, it is just as true of positive feedback. Just as we are inhibited about telling people what we dislike about their behaviour, we seem equally reluctant to tell them what we appreciate about them.

When you are working with a client group you are likely to pick up a lot of data about how people perceive each other. In the security of an interview, with guarantees of confidentiality, they are likely to share their perceptions and feelings about colleagues, other departments, their boss, senior managers, etc.—sometimes positive, sometimes negative. It would be helpful if there was some kind of mechanism for sharing this data with each other and the others being discussed. Of course, it is inevitable that you, too, will have perceptions and feelings about the way your clients behave towards you.

It follows, therefore, that another dilemma facing you as an internal consultant is how to help members of your client system give each other, and you, constructive feedback on their perceptions of each other, and how to share your own perceptions of individual clients. This is obviously a delicate issue and handled badly it could do more harm than good. There are several important points to remember when giving feedback to others or facilitating the process during which people give each other feedback.

First of all it is absolutely essential that people give each other feedback in an environment where they feel valued. If all I receive is information about what I do badly then my confidence is likely to be undermined and I am less likely to act on the information. If on the other hand I know that you like me and value me, and I know what you appreciate about me, I tend to be much more receptive when you give me negative feedback. So always start by talking about, or getting others to talk about, all the things they value about the recipient of the feedback. This helps recipients to put any negative feedback in context while not discounting what is said about them.

If feedback is to be helpful it should always be given with care. This means that it is given out of a genuine desire to help the recipient. Helpful feedback is not given to avenge some real or imagined slight or to get even but to offer some valuable information which may help others reflect on their behaviour and think of ways they might prefer to behave. One feedback exercise we use is called 'Our Gift to You' (see Chapter 3, Exercise 3) simply because feedback, when given with care and generosity, is just that, a valuable gift.

Personal feedback is of no value if it is not honest. This is not to say it has to be 'brutally honest'. You should never be brutal. But if you are withholding information from clients you may be doing them a disservice. Feedback should also be immediate; telling me how you feel about something I have just done is more helpful than telling me how you felt about something I did yesterday, last week or last year!

Feedback needs to be clear. We often hear people who resist giving feedback say that they get it and give it 'all the time' through tone of voice and gestures. But non-verbal feedback needs to be interpreted and there's no guarantee that the message we receive is the one being given. Even verbally it is often difficult to find exactly the words we are looking for, and even then the words may have different meanings to the recipient from the ones that were intended. Words need to be chosen carefully: describe the behaviour and the feelings you have, and then check to find out what the recipient has actually heard.

Finally, remember that when you give someone personal feedback it is never 'the truth'. It is simply your perception, and your perception may or may not be shared by others. For example, a sense of humour which you find attractive may be irritating to others. Do encourage the recipient to check out any feedback he or she receives with other people to get a clearer, and perhaps more balanced, picture.

Giving personal feedback and encouraging others to give it can be very difficult. It involves a high degree of commitment, emotional involvement and risk. It is often counter to the culture and mythology of the organization. Very often people need to overcome tremendous inhibitions in order to start giving feedback at all. But in the end if we can help people see themselves as others do we have done them a great personal service. (For a summary of the essential points about giving personal feedback see Checklist 6.3 at the end of the chapter.)

Summary

- Gathering data which relates solely to your technical discipline is likely to ignore important elements of organizational problems.
- Exotic data such as feelings and intuition is often ignored, but is always present in any assignment.
- Making sense of complex data often requires organizational models, such as the organization diagnostic model and the group working model.

- The organization diagnostic model divides activites into six inter-dependent areas:
  - Purpose and Tasks
  - Structure
  - People
  - Rewards
  - Procedures
  - Technology
- The group working model uses three categories:
  - task
  - systems and procedures
  - process
- Data can be gathered through:
  - interviews
  - questionnaires
  - direct observation
  - document analysis
  - your own experience and intuition
- Helpful questioning could include:
  - open-ended questions
  - supplementary questions
  - clarifying questions
  - reflecting
  - asking about feelings
  - forecasting or 'fantasy' questions
- Less helpful questions include:
  - leading questions
  - multiple choice questions
  - embroidered questions
  - unanswerable questions
  - statements posing as questions
- Providing feedback is a crucial phase in the consulting process, and is essential for development and progress.
- Both positive and negative feedback are of value but must always be constructive.
- Feedback should be given as an assignment is progressing as well as at the end. Saving all the feedback for a final feedback meeting is a recipe for disaster.
- Personal feedback needs to be given with care and in an environment where the recipient feels valued.
- Remember, feedback is never 'the truth', it is simply your perception.

Exercises

1 Why are clients reluctant to deal with process issues?

Earlier in this chapter we asked you to list all the reasons you could think of why clients may be reluctant to work on process problems. Below is our list. It's not intended to be definitive by any means and we are sure you will have thought of a lot of reasons that we didn't.

- Exploring process issues is messy and ambiguous.
- It can feel very personal and uncomfortable, even threatening.
- People often think that if they acknowledge the existence of a process problem, they may be opening a Pandora's box.
- It is difficult to control.
- No one knows where it will lead.
- Once the problem is out in the open it can no longer be ignored.
- Dealing with process issues may be seen as the responsibility of the personnel or training department.
- Dealing with process issues involves acknowledging people's feelings and it usually isn't legitimate to share feelings at work.
- People often believe that they are not competent to deal with other people's feelings.
- There is often a myth that 'stress is good for people'.
- It is seen as prying into personal affairs.
- 'We have quality people—they can cope.'
- Process issues are often embodied in the culture of the organization and include a lot of widely believed myths, e.g. about what can and can't be said.

2 Using your intuition as a source of data

You can often collect a lot of data about a new client group simply by being aware of your own feelings and reactions. This can tell you a lot about what it's like to work in the group. Earlier in the chapter we asked you to generate a list of questions you might ask yourself in order to draw on intuitive data. Below is our list—once again it is not meant to be definitive.

- How do I feel? Comfortable? Uncomfortable? Threatened? etc.
- What is the atmosphere like? Polite? Friendly? Strained?
- Is there an air of formality or informality?
- How welcome do I feel?
- Who talks to me?
- Who ignores me?
- How am I treated?
- How is the boss treated? With deference? As an equal? With respect?
- How inhibited do I feel about raising the possibility of process issues?
- Do I feel listened to or not listened to?
- Who talks to whom?
- Who gets ignored?
- What kind of humour prevails? Is it sarcastic? Are there lots of in-jokes? Are there lots of put-downs? Is it gentle humour? Is it supportive?
- Do I feel comfortable or uncomfortable with the humour?
- Are women treated differently from men? Women consultants can often get an enormous amount of data about gender issues which is less obvious or unavailable to men.
- How open or closed are people with the information they give me?

Checklist 6.1 *Gathering organizational and exotic data*

When gathering data you might ask the following questions:

- What is the presenting problem?
- How clear are different members of this client system about the common objective to which they all contribute?
- How do they get agreement on resources needed to achieve their objective?
- What are the formal organizational relationships between members of the system?
- What are the formal communication channels? How effective are they?
- What do your own feelings tell you about what it might be like to work here?
- What kind of humour is prevalent? Is it supportive? Is it ritualistic? Are there a lot of put-downs?
- How does the boss operate? How do people behave when the boss is around?
- What are people open about and what doesn't get talked about?
- How are decisions made?
- Who participates in decisions? Who gets listened to? Who gets ignored?
- How is disagreement managed?
- How empowered or powerless do people feel?
- Are feelings discussed openly?

Checklist 6.2 *Managing the feedback meeting*

Some ideas on what data to use and what not to use:

- The clients have a right to all the information you have collected.
- You probably will not use all the data you have collected so trust your intuition and provide enough to give a clear picture of the situation as you found it.
- Include data which confirms success not just failure.
- Remember which information was provided on a confidential basis, which has to be reported anonymously and which may be freely and openly discussed.
- Include data that calls attention to the real problem as well as the presenting problem where you see these as different.
- Don't hide data which may be uncomfortable for the client to face.
- Highlight data which refers to what the client has authority and responsibility to change.
- Use data to highlight a manageable number of problems or aspects of a problem.
- Include data which is likely to be seen as important and calls attention to problems where there is commitment to change.

Some ideas on how to present the data and how not to do it:

- Don't overload the client with detail. Consign as much of it as possible to an appendix if you must put it somewhere.
- Go easy on historical data—the client will most certainly know more about it than you do.
- Support the client while you are giving feedback by emphasizing what is going well and being encouraging about the future.
- Be prepared to confront the client. Reactions may be uncomfortable but they are part of your job. If you are not prepared to confront, why have you been hired?
- Be aware of the limits of what your *client* can accept—don't let your own feelings be projected onto the client. Don't leave out data because you wouldn't like to hear it.
- Don't collude by allowing the client to put the blame on others or on circumstances beyond his or her control.
- Remember the guidelines for effective feedback. Feedback is about 'what is', not 'what should be'. Feedback which the client receives as aggressive or non-assertive is likely to raise resistance or be ignored.
- Say clearly and concisely what problems you see without implying that the management is at fault—don't judge or evaluate.
- Be aware of the process issues during the meeting—deal with resistance as it happens and share your own feelings when appropriate.
- Feedback doesn't need to be one-way—from consultant to client. If you have been working together well, the client will have some idea of what the problems are and what to do about them.

Some ideas on how to structure the feedback meeting to achieve results:

- However much data you present and however many recommendations you make nothing will happen without client commitment.
- Your recommendations need to be tied to some aspect or aspects of the problem and point to some expected benefits.
- You need the client to take responsibility for the recommendations and own them—ensure that they are manageable and achievable.
- Try to ensure that all those involved in implementation receive the feedback. (Remember the definition of a client system—'Who knows, Who can, Who cares'.)
- The following structure might help with the meeting:
  - Restate the original contract
  - State purpose and structure of the meeting
  - Agree the agenda
  - Present the data in simple form
  - Present the diagnosis of the problem
  - Get reactions to diagnosis
  - Present recommendations, implications and benefits
  - Get reactions to recommendations
  - Get decision to implement
- Finally, stay in control of the meeting, keep the client focused on

action to deal with the problem and keep most of the time for discussion.

Checklist 6.3   *Giving personal feedback*

Effective feedback is:

- given in a climate in which people value each other
- balanced between positive points and negative points
- for the benefit of the recipient, not the giver
- honest
- given close to the event
- clearly expressed in language the recipient can understand
- non-judgemental
- a description of the recipient's behaviour and the emotion of the giver
- requested by the recipient
- constructive
- checked out with others
- given in a way that leaves the recipient free to choose whether or not to take it on board
- timely

7 Making sense of the data— problem diagnosis and decision making

The nature of problems

Before we examine the issues of problem diagnosis it is important to acknowledge, at the outset, that the word 'problem' can create difficulties. It is hard to think of an alternative word—'issue', perhaps, although it sounds rather like jargon. So why is 'problem' such an inappropriate word? People often find it difficult to acknowledge that they have problems. The word can suggest that the individuals are in some way inadequate, ineffective and unable to cope. To 'have a problem' suggests that the owners are powerless to solve it themselves and are therefore dependent on someone else. This kind of thinking leads us to assume that there is something wrong with needing help, and makes it less likely that we will ask for help when we need it.

It may be something of a platitude now to think in terms of opportunities rather than problems. But if you are to be effective it is probably best to help the client define the problem in optimistic rather than pessimistic terms. After all, we need help with the good things in life as well as the bad. If we are planning a holiday we need help to decide on the best place to go, and when, where to stay and how to get there. If we have spare money we don't shrink from seeking help from a financial adviser to help us decide where to invest it. So the word 'problem' doesn't have to have negative connotations.

If clients want to improve it doesn't mean that what they were doing was wrong, just that they want their operation to be even more effective and run more smoothly than it does at present. The other disadvantage of the word 'problem' is that people often imagine that for every problem there must be a solution or a correct answer. This kind of thinking probably has its roots in traditional education where students did indeed deal with correct answers. We all learned how to add two and two, the date of the Battle of Hastings, the capital of Australia and the chemical formula for water. It comes as a shock to find that when we leave the confines of academia the problems we face in the rest of our lives are rarely as neat as these. It is useful to distinguish between *puzzles*, which have a best answer, and *problems*, for which there are lots of alternative courses of action, none of which will 'solve' the problem in the sense of it going away. Education usually presents us with puzzles while life confronts us with problems which are messy and ambiguous and where there is never a right answer. Getting through a maze, solving a Rubik cube or doing a jigsaw are all puzzles, while 'how to motivate the sales force' or 'how to balance the budget' are problems. When dealing with problems there is never a ten-out-of-ten solution. Rather you may be trying to help your clients choose between several four-out-of-ten options. Having decided on the option to take there will be no way of knowing for sure if it was better or worse than any of the others we didn't choose.

When you are working with clients there may well be aspects of the assignment which are indeed puzzles. The OR consultant can use mathematical models which can help a manager decide on the most cost-effective course of action. However, when it comes to selling the consequent changes to the work force so that they are committed to them, you are firmly in the realms of problems to which there can never be a perfect solution.

When helping clients to examine the data that has been collected and make decisions about the way forward it is important to differentiate between the presenting problem and the underlying real problem. Often the problem may appear to be concerned with systems and procedures but so often the real problem, or at least part of the real problem, is to do with process.

For example, on one occasion we were involved in what looked on the surface like a straightforward office reorganization problem. A department of about thirty people was divided into two groups. The operational group was responsible for working on a number of projects with their clients, mostly in other organizations. This role was subject to a lot of pressure and instant decisions, and members of this group were frequently out of the office. The other group provided a research and information service to the operational people. The quality of this service was crucial to the success of the department as a whole. The large open-plan office contained the whole department but the operational people occupied one half and the research people the other. Between them had been erected a wall of filing cabinets and cupboards which contributed to the isolation of the two groups. So the presenting problem seemed to be how to rearrange the office to maximize contact between the two groups. Further research revealed, however, that this was only part of the problem. The department had undergone a period of very rapid growth and had taken on new responsibilities which had led to a lack of clarity about individual responsibilities. The research group tended to recruit people who had an eye for detail, rational analysis and caution, while the operational group was largely composed of extroverts, who enjoyed managing crises and making instant decisions. Both sides consequently tended to devalue the other's strengths rather than recognize that they were complementary. They tended to blame each other rather than collaborate. The operational group would fail to involve the research group early enough in a project, and would request urgent information in a piecemeal way, leading to frustration on both sides.

The erection of the barrier between the two groups exacerbated the problem but it seemed to be rather more a symptom of an underlying problem of two groups of very different people trying (or perhaps not trying) to work together. The problem was redefined as one of helping people in the group to value each other's contribution, recognize how their strengths complemented each other and work together in a more collaborative way.

A useful way of categorizing organizational problems was developed by Blake and Mouton (1976, 1983) in their book *Consultation*. They identified four possible 'focal issues' which may be worked on by the consultant and client. These are:

- power–authority
- morale–cohesion
- norms–standards
- goals–objectives

Blake and Mouton suggested that all organizational problems have underlying issues that fall into one or more of these four categories. Power–authority seems to be the most frequent focal issue, centring around the location and use or misuse of power in an organization, its management style, and often a resulting feeling of powerlessness among employees. Morale–cohesion problems focus on how people feel in the organization, how motivated they are, whether they feel important, and whether they feel they are consulted about decisions. Often, in times of change, there are repercussions about morale and cohesion in the organization. Sometimes you may find yourself helping clients to re-examine their norms and standards—how things are done round here. This includes what is considered appropriate and inappropriate behaviour: does everyone leave at the normal finishing time, for example, or is it the norm to work late? Often a change in technology can only be success-ful if there is an accompanying change in working patterns—a change in norms and standards. The fourth focal issue you may need to work on concerns goals and objectives. You could be involved with helping a team to identify what it's really trying to achieve or helping it come to terms with the fact that the goals have actually changed. With changes in financial legislation, for example, most financial institutions have had to broaden the definitions of their goals and objectives. Building societies, for example, are no longer in the business of simply arranging home loans but now offer a much broader range of services.

Blake and Mouton point out that these focal issues are interdependent. If you are working in one area it is important to look out for the effects in another area. If an organization is expanding rapidly, for example, there are likely to be difficulties in each focal issue. As the organization grows the managers are likely to become more remote and a manage-ment style suitable for a small organization may not be appropriate any more. The objectives of the organization may become blurred as it takes on more products, services or projects. As new people arrive they are likely to challenge existing norms and standards and, finally, those who remember the time when the business was small and exciting may feel resentful or diminished as individuals as they see the organization growing around them.

So you need to remember to help your clients look at problems in a positive way while at the same time discouraging them from expecting you to wave a magic wand. Real problems rarely lend themselves to perfect solutions. However, it will help if you can try to identify the real problem rather than simply working with the apparent problem.

Making sense of process data

Sometimes teams are unable to complete their task because they have inadequate resources or do not have the required skills. There are also situations where the task does not get done because of inadequate policies and procedures, poor organization or lack of a proper definition of roles and responsibilities. However, it is often more likely that the real reason for not getting the task done is a process one, such as poor power/authority relationships, lack of understanding about goals and objectives, inappropriate norms and standards, or strong feelings about the organization or its management which are producing severe morale/cohesion problems. Such process issues are hard to surface and difficult to deal with for a variety of reasons which were discussed in Chapter 6.

A frequent dilemma faced by consultants is: 'Do I stay at the felt-needs level or take a more direct line?' Often the client will be aware of the real needs and may take a poor view of a consultant who doesn't identify them. Process consultation might help you to surface process difficulties so that the client has a better understanding of the real needs.

With some understanding of what is likely to happen in groups at a process level it is possible for a skilled consultant to observe what is going on and feed back the observations to the group. Such observations can alert group members to what they are doing or not doing which is preventing them from getting their task done satisfactorily.

These include:

Participation   Who are high participators, who are low? How are silent people treated? Who talks to whom? Who leads? Who keeps the ball rolling?

Influence   Who is high in influence, who is low? Is there any rivalry in the group? Is the boss more influential than the team members?

Styles of influence   How do people influence others? Do they use rewards and punishments, common vision, assertive persuasion or participation and trust?

Sensitivity to feelings   Do members of the group notice when people are ignored, interrupted or talked over? Do they do anything about it or merely ignore it? Do they ask each other how they are feeling?

Dealing with issues as they arise   Does the group recognize when members are upset, in difficulty or not saying what they feel?

Conflict handling   How does the group handle differences of opinion? Do they avoid all conflict, handle it to reach agreement collaboratively, constantly compromise or end up with a slanging match?

Group atmosphere   What is it like? Friendly and cosy, quiet and demotivating, noisy and argumentative? Do you get the feeling that there are hidden agendas around? Do you get the impression that the trust level is low?

These are some of the many aspects of group process which you can help group members to look at with a view to improving their relationships and therefore the way they work together.

So how do you go about helping a client group to identify process issues which are blocking the effectiveness of the group?

First of all, it is important to have a high level of entry with the group and a clear contract. Group members are unlikely to open up and discuss difficult, perhaps painful issues with a consultant who is not equally open and whom they do not trust. Equally, it is important that group members are involved in the diagnosis of the process problem(s) and explicitly contract to explore the issues and deal with them.

The role of the consultant is to help clients find techniques for identifying and surfacing process issues and then help them to decide what group actions and behaviours need to be improved. Clients will be much more committed to improving the way they work together if they decide themselves what needs to be done.

A prescriptive approach to process consultation is unlikely to be successful. If you simply observe the group, and identify what you see as the problem, you are likely to miss all the significant things that are happening in the group which simply can't be seen: the issues that are being avoided, for example, or how people are feeling about the way the group works. In addition, if you feed back your observations to the group and prescribe what must be done to improve, the people in the group are likely to feel criticized and become defensive. They will reject the feedback and you may find yourself under attack.

A more appropriate style for process interventions is catalytic. It is much more effective to ask questions that help members of the client group explore their own perceptions of what is happening in the group and listen to the perceptions of others. There are two ways of helping with this exploration. One is simply to put questions to the group and help them deal with the issues that surface. Process questions might include:

- How are decisions made in this group?
- Who are the high and low participators in this group?
- How did group members feel when a specific event occurred?
- What are the major areas of conflict in the group?

A second way is to ask group members to complete questionnaires or feedback instruments about group effectiveness and then share the results of such surveys. You need to help the group deal with similarities and differences in the way the instruments are completed.

At the end of the chapter you will find a number of feedback instruments which can be used to help clients focus on process data.

Whatever method of process intervention you use it is important to remember that the purpose is to help the clients identify and diagnose the problem and then make decisions about what they want to do about it.

As a process consultant you have several advantages over the group members:

- You do not share the same pressures felt by ordinary members to be loyal to the group and stay the same.
- You can more easily focus attention on procedures, processes and relationships.
- You are not likely to be involved in power, leadership or formal authority relationships as members of the group often are.
- You are not likely to be party to participant-centred frictions, antagonisms and cliques.
- Consultants, by virtue of their interventionist role, are membership-free.

However, this may put the internal process consultant under even more pressure if he or she tries to give feedback to the group which they perceive as critical, evaluative or judgemental. So if you want the group to use the feedback—prescription is out.

Decision making

We often think that an absence of information prevents us from making decisions. This may be true but in organizations the opposite can also be the case. A manager may well be made impotent simply because there is too much data about the problem. The most helpful thing that you can do in this situation is provide ways of clarifying, simplifying or restructuring the data so that the clients are able to understand the dimensions of the problem more clearly and can decide what they want to do about it. If you are going to help your clients in this way it is important that you have access to a few decision-making models which are designed to clarify the problem and what needs to be done. You may have such models as part of your normal technical expertise, like, for example, discounted cash flow, cost benefit analysis, critical examination, or algorithms. Indeed, all consulting professions have their own techniques for making decisions. These can be used prescriptively to solve clients' problems or catalytically to help them make sense of their own data and make their own decisions.

Two simple but very useful models which can help clients clarify their understanding of problems and make decisions are decision trees and force field analysis. The decision tree method is a way of helping clients look at all the data about the problem systemically, clarify its nature and then identify possible options and examine them objectively. The force field method can be used with any situation of change, from one facing an individual to a complex organizational problem where there are lots of process issues which can't be controlled directly but which need to be worked on over a period of time.

Decision trees

There are many forms of decision trees which can be used for problem solving. The approach we prefer was developed by Paul Sargent (*A Decision Tree Approach to Case Study Solution*, NEBSM, 1979) as a means of imposing structure and logic on what is often a sea of ambiguity. It is called a decision 'tree' simply because when it is complete its shape bears a strong resemblance to a tree with a trunk, roots, branches, twigs and fruit (see Figure 7.1).

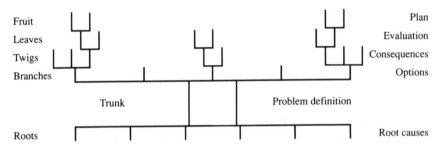

Figure 7.1 *Schematic diagram of a decision tree*
Source: Paul B. Sargent, *A Decision Tree Approach to Case Study Solution*, NEBSM, 1979. Reproduced by permission of the publisher.

Statement of the problem

A crucial stage in problem solving is defining the problem and it may be necessary to go back to this point several times before progress can be made. It is important at this stage to differentiate:

- the presenting problem
- the symptoms
- the real problem

It is important to ensure that the clients are actually tackling the real problem, otherwise they will find that an excellent solution is being produced for the wrong problem. Clients will begin with the presenting problem and this will often be described in terms of systems and procedures: 'We're not reaching targets', 'We're not keeping to budgets', 'Quality is falling', etc.

The danger is always to rush into possible solutions immediately without clarifying and redefining the problem. The best thing at this stage is to go back to examine the background and root causes.

Root causes of the problem

An examination of the background to the problem is likely to expose the fact that at least part of the problem is caused by human process factors as well as technical, systems and procedures factors. A fall in quality may be caused by a lowering of morale due to an inappropriate management style or to an inability to communicate effectively with suppliers. Failure to meet sales targets might owe as much to poor training as to the low quality of the product.

An exploration of the root causes of the problem will give clues to the appropriate definition of the real problem as well as possible solutions.

Redefining the problem

Having explored the background to the problem you will be in a better position to redefine the problem and crystallize the real problem (or problems). The important thing at this stage is to make certain that the problem is redefined in such a way as to ensure that the clients own the problem and are prepared to take responsibility for it. You should discourage clients from defining the problem in a way that places blame and responsibility on other people.

'The problem is that people just aren't interested.'
'My boss is incompetent.'
'The department is just too big.'
'The sales territory is too small.'

As long as clients persist in defining the problem in a way that creates distance from themselves, it will be difficult to get commitment. One way of ensuring client ownership is to ask them to define the problem in a short phrase or sentence starting with the words 'how to'. Instead of talking about how incompetent the boss is, ask clients to redefine the problem starting with the words 'how to'. A few redefinitions might include:

'How to give my boss some feedback'
'How to persuade my boss that I want to be involved in decisions which affect my job'
'How to help my boss to delegate better'
'How to arrange a meeting where my boss and I can discuss the way we work together in an open way'
'How to get another job'

Redefining the problem in this way ensures that when you start generating possible solutions you will at least be trying to solve the problem that the clients want to work on.

Generating alternative solutions

Having clearly defined the problem or problems the next step is to explore any options that may be available. Try to generate as many options as possible without considering the arguments for or against. Also ensure that no option is rejected at this stage. If several 'real' problems are identified, you may need to produce a separate list of options for each problem.

Evaluating the options   The next stage is to evaluate each option in turn. To do this means asking such questions as:

- Would this option help to solve the problem as it has been redefined?
- What would be the consequences of taking this option?
- What are the costs and benefits?
- What are the advantages and disadvantages?
- How do you feel about that option? Often an option can look like the logical thing to do, but there may be lots of emotional barriers.

By evaluating all the options in this way it will become evident that some options can be rejected while others might point the way forward. Furthermore, it is important to recognize at this stage that there is rarely a simple neat solution that will 'solve' the problem. More likely you will be looking at a combination of options which are likely to improve the situation rather than provide an everlasting solution.

Taking action   Identifying the option or options which seem to be appropriate is not the end of the line. It is now necessary to work out a detailed action plan of what needs to be done in order to implement the selected option(s). To do this you need to ask questions like these:

- What do you need to do first?
- Then what needs to happen?
- How do you need to prepare for that?
- When does that need to happen by?
- What reactions might you get?

By doing this you are increasing client commitment to implementing the action plan.

Using a decision tree approach   It is possible to use the decision tree approach in two ways:

- as a way of exploring a problem with clients (Figure 7.1 on page 140)
- as a way of presenting clients with the content of a complex investigation (Figure 7.2)

The decision tree can be used as a framework for asking questions to help clients explore the problem, define it and generate possible solutions. By asking a series of structured questions clients are enabled to structure their own decision tree and work from confusion to a degree of clarity. Let us see how this works in practice. Choose a problem you have at the moment and try to answer the following questions:

1 *The trunk*
   Give a brief description of the problem as you see it now (trunk).

2 *The roots*
   Who else is involved in the problem?
   How do you feel about the other people involved in the problem?
   What are the technical aspects of the problem?
   How is the problem being managed at the moment?
   What do you see as the symptoms of the problem?

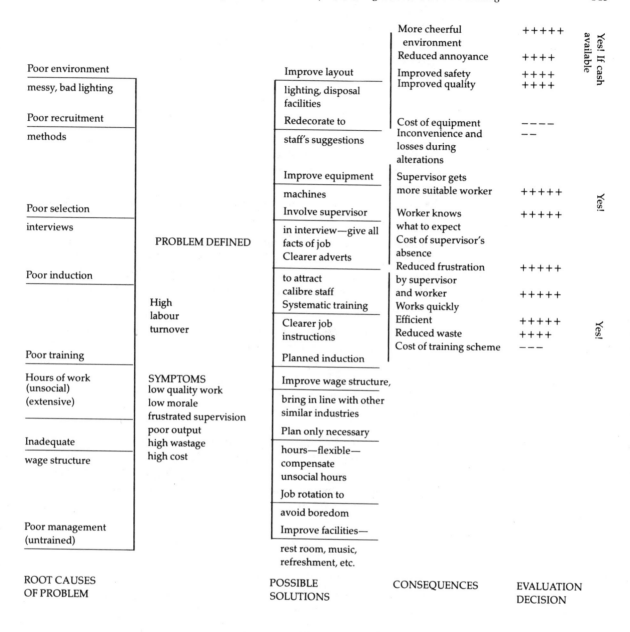

Figure 7.2 *Example of a decision tree*

What difficulties does the problem cause you?
How important is it to you to solve the problem?
What do you see as the root causes of the problem?

3 *Back to the trunk*
Can you now redefine your problem in a single sentence starting with the words 'how to . . .'?

4 *The branches*

What options are available to you? Write down as many options as you can think of. Don't evaluate any of them.

5 *The twigs*

Now take each of the options you have identified and answer the following questions:

- What are the advantages and benefits?
- What are the disadvantages and costs?
- What will be the other likely consequences?
- How do you feel about this option?
- To what extent does this option solve the problem redefined by you?

6 *The fruit*

Which option or options seem to have the greatest chance of success? Now plan how you will implement the option. First write down all the actions you need to carry out in the order you need to do them. Then write dates against each one to indicate when you intend to have it completed.

We believe this exercise indicates that it is possible to help clients construct their own decision tree even though you have very little understanding of the technicalities or details of the problem. The purpose of the technique is to help the clients understand the problem rather than to understand it yourself. Having clarified the problem in this way, clients are better able to move into decision making with confidence.

Presenting data to the client

Sometimes, having completed a detailed investigation for a client, you may need to present the results in report form. If the report is long or complex, then using a decision tree is a very effective way of presenting the dimensions of the investigation in a way which is readily understood. Figure 7.2 gives an example.

Force field analysis

Some years ago Kurt Lewin developed a set of ideas in sociology called 'field theory' (1951). One of his ideas, the force field analysis, is a simple but extremely useful technique for exploring problems and developing strategies for change. His ideas have been modified and developed over the years but the basic framework has stood the test of time.

The first step in the force field process is to describe the problem as it is now, and then desribe how you would like the situation to be in the future. For example, someone exploring the problem of morale might describe the present and future situations in the manner shown in Table 7.1.

Force field analysis suggests there are two sets of forces working in the system. One set of forces is driving towards the desired goal while the other set is pushing in the opposite direction (Table 7.2). When these forces are in equilibrium then no change will occur.

Table 7.1

Present situation	Desired future situation
Low morale	*High morale*
• high absence • people unconcerned about quality • resentment of managers • 'us' and 'them' outlook • low cooperation • work needs to be closely inspected • few ideas from staff • poor communication between sections	• low absence • people concerned about quality of their work • collaborative relationship between staff and manager • lots of ideas coming from the staff • staff take responsibility for discussing and working on problems with colleagues

Table 7.2

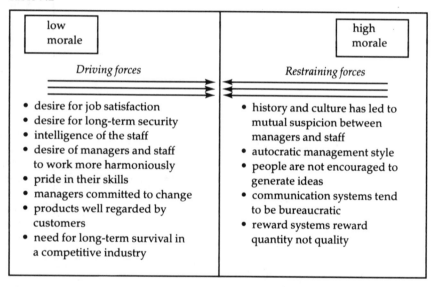

low morale	high morale
Driving forces	*Restraining forces*
• desire for job satisfaction • desire for long-term security • intelligence of the staff • desire of managers and staff to work more harmoniously • pride in their skills • managers committed to change • products well regarded by customers • need for long-term survival in a competitive industry	• history and culture has led to mutual suspicion between managers and staff • autocratic management style • people are not encouraged to generate ideas • communication systems tend to be bureaucratic • reward systems reward quantity not quality

The advantage of using a 'force field' on a problem is that it now becomes more manageable. If we simply describe the current situation and the desired future situation then the gulf between them appears huge. There is no simple solution and no clear way to manage the change. However, when we list the driving forces and restraining forces we begin to clarify ways in which we can actually influence the system and facilitate the change. We can take positive action either to strengthen the driving forces or reduce the restraining forces. However, there is a danger in expending too much energy trying to reduce the power of the restraining forces. You are likely to get more effective change by working with the people who want it rather than the people who don't.

In the example cited in Table 7.2 we can pick out some of the drivers and restrainers that can be influenced.

Table 7.3

Driving/restraining forces	*What can be done*
• desire for long-term security	• communicate long- and short-term plans to the workforce
• desire for job satisfaction	• communicate past and current successes
	• encourage staff to generate ideas for improvement. Make sure ideas are listened to and acted on
	• involve staff in making decisions
	• work on ways of delegating more responsibility
	• introduce a system of briefing groups
	• introduce quality circles, problem-solving groups or task forces
• desire of managers and staff to work more harmoniously	• team building
	• give the team opportunities to talk through the way they work together
	• group to work on clear department and individual goals and objectives
• autocratic management style	• organization development programme during which managers examine their management style and the implications for the business

Force field analysis is a very effective model to use with clients when they are facing change which seems too large, unmanageable and difficult to control. In this situation clients can feel powerless because they can't see the 'solution' to the problem. However, using a force field can bring the problem into focus and help them to recognize that, while there may not be a simple solution, there are actions they can take which can influence the problem. So you end up with empowered clients.

Using theories and models

As we have already seen there are many ways of organizing complex data so that it becomes manageable. Using a decision tree and a force field are two ways of doing this. Another way is to use theories and models as a means of helping clients to understand the nature of the problem. This is, after all, how we make sense of the world around us and make decisions on a daily basis. If I throw a ball in the air and watch it fall to the ground I can understand, describe and predict what will happen on future occasions through the theory of gravity. When driving a car, the decisions we make are based on a number of theories and models—relative speed, for example, and the convention that everyone will drive on the correct side of the road.

All consultants have available to them a range of theories, models and conventions which are part of their technical expertise. Consultants may use these theories and models to identify clients' problems and solve them. They see their superior knowledge as a guarantee of future employment. However, the danger of this approach is that it creates client dependence. We often hear stories about consultants who introduce a new system and then stick around for months or even years because they are the only ones who know how the system works.

It is easy to fall into the trap of jealously guarding this expertise as a source of power. In contrast, client-centred consultants try to empower their clients by sharing their knowledge and expertise. When you are working on a problem with clients you can share some of your expertise so that your clients are enabled to make the decisions. In this way your clients can not only decide what to do about the current problem but will be able to tackle future problems themselves. The old adage is certainly true: if you give a starving man a fish you feed him for a day; if you teach him to fish you feed him for life.

Soon after establishing his business one of the authors went to see his accountant with a pile of receipts, invoice copies and VAT demands, in a state of general confusion. It would have been possible (and lucrative) for the accountant simply to ask the author to send all future invoices and statements to him so that he could prepare the accounts. Instead, a thirty-minute lesson in basic double entry book-keeping meant the author was henceforth able to handle that side of the business himself. It was not necessary for the accountant to provide a lot of theory. The author certainly did not need to be turned into an accountant, he just needed enough theory to help him become more organized and keep his own basic books.

What then is the best way of enabling clients to learn and use theories and models that will help them to become more effective? Traditional educationalists have often used the 'mug and jug' approach to learning. They see learning as merely passing on knowledge from the expert (the jug) into the brain of the learner (the mug). The assumption is that learning can be passed from one person to another. This often results in classrooms of unenthusiastic pupils being lectured on theories which they are expected to learn and then implement. Unfortunately, this approach is also quite common among trainers in organizations, who develop courses that involve 'teaching' participants a number of theories chosen by the trainer which the participants are then expected to take back to the workplace and use. In our experience this transfer of learning rarely takes place.

In order to recognize why this approach fails, we need to understand what differentiates a useful theory from one that is not so useful. At this stage it may help to identify two theories that you have been taught at some time in your life. Choose one that you still understand and is clear to you and one which remains only a hazy memory, the detail forgotten. Write in Table 7.4 why you remembered one and forgot the other.

Table 7.4

A theory that remains clear *Characteristics*	A theory that has become hazy *Characteristics*

When describing theories they have found useful, people often make statements like these:

- It was well taught in the first place.
- I could see its relevance when I learnt it.
- It helped me understand my own behaviour/failures/successes/ difficulties, etc.
- I have been able to convert the theory into practice and use it.
- I feel confident in using the theory.
- It has stood the test of time.

We can conclude that in order to be useful a theory must help the client understand the problem and make effective decisions both now and in the future.

Learning cycle

As we saw in Chapter 1, Kolb recognized that the learning process can be developed into a cyclical model of learning, and suggested that internalizing new learning requires the learner to engage in all stages of the learning cycle (see Figure 7.3).

Concrete experience

The learning process usually starts with the learner's own experience. The learner becomes involved in an activity, acts or behaves in some way, performs, observes, says something. This experience is the basis for the entire learning process.

Reflective observation

The experience itself generates a lot of data. The learner or learners will be left with a variety of feelings and memories of the event. The learner now needs to reflect on the experience in order to make sense of it, to understand what happened and why, and to come to terms with his or her own feelings about the event. To do this it is necessary to answer questions like these:

- What happened and in what sequence?
- How did it feel?

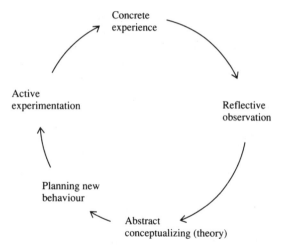

Figure 7.3   *The experiential learning cycle*

- What did the learner do?
- What did the other people involved do?
- What was said?
- How did others react?
- What worked? Why?
- What didn't work? Why?
- How could the situation have been handled differently?

The process of reflection helps the individual understand events that have taken place and increases the possibility of learning from them.

Abstract conceptualization   This is the stage of conceptualizing and theorizing when the learner develops general principles from the experience which are applicable to other situations. In other words, the learner starts to develop his or her own theory which can be used to make decisions in the future.

Planning new behaviour   The next step is to plan new behaviour based on the theory which has been developed. This is a crucial phase in the cycle because it is not until this stage that the learner begins to think in terms of changing and actually doing things differently.

Active experimentation   Kolb's model is cyclical so that as soon as the learner moves to active experimentation to put the plan into action and try out new behaviour, then he or she moves quickly back into the experiencing phase. This leads to reflecting on the success of the new behaviour, modifying the theory if necessary and then deciding if further change in behaviour is required. Eventually, after several trips round the cycle, the theory and the behaviour become internalized. This means that they become part of the individual and can be accessed at an automatic or unconscious level.

A good example of the learning cycle in action is learning to drive a car. Learning to drive is a continuous process of experimentation with attendant successes and failures, followed by gradually increasing understanding and skill. At first all the actions involved are done at a very conscious, usually uncomfortable, level. Gradually, however, the driver internalizes all the behaviour until eventually most drivers operate their cars at an unconscious level.

As we saw in Chapter 1, it is important to acknowledge at this point that different people have different learning styles. This means that we all have a preference for the activities associated with one or more phases of the learning cycle; it could also mean that we underutilize the others.

So how can you use this learning cycle to help someone to learn? It is possible to break into the cycle with either the experience or the theory. Let us look at an example. If you are a sales manager helping a sales executive to build skills in closing the sale, you can do this in several ways. The first way is to accompany the sales executive on a number of calls on customers (the experience). After the calls you could spend some time discussing them and how the sales executive operated, why some sales were successful and some weren't (reflection). At this point you could introduce a theory of closing the sale. This can be done in two ways. One way is to explain the sales executive's success and failures in terms of your theory of closing the sale. The other option is to help the sales executive generate his or her own theory. This can be done by asking such questions as: 'So what do you think is important when closing the sale?'

Finally, you would need to help the sales executive think through how to close the sale on the next call. At this point the whole process starts all over again until eventually the theories and skills become internalized and automatic (see Figure 7.4).

The second option is to start with the theory. This would involve introducing the salesperson to the theory of closing the sale and ensuring a good level of intellectual understanding (theory). You would then need to help your client to plan how he or she can implement the theory when calling on customers (planning new behaviour). Next you accompany the salesperson while he or she calls on customers and practises the new behaviour (experience) and afterwards you discuss the calls with the salesperson (reflection). During this discussion you help the client identify how successful he or she was in doing what was intended and how it felt, while also giving additional feedback. Again it will be necessary to continue round the learning cycle until theory and behaviour have been internalized (see Figure 7.5).

We discussed in Chapter 1 the striking similarity between Kolb's learning styles model and the consulting cycle. This is not surprising because, as a consultant, you are in the business of helping people change their behaviour, that is, helping them to learn. Figure 7.6 shows that the introduction of theories and models can help the client to make sense of the data and make decisions. But, as we have seen in Kolb's basic learning styles model, the trainer or coach must decide when to introduce the theory—before or after the experience of the learner.

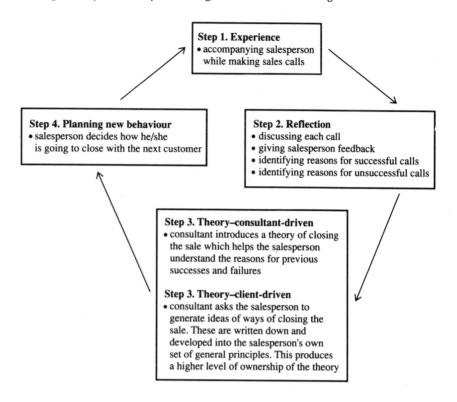

Figure 7.4 *Using the learning cycle to build sales closing skills: starting with the client's data*

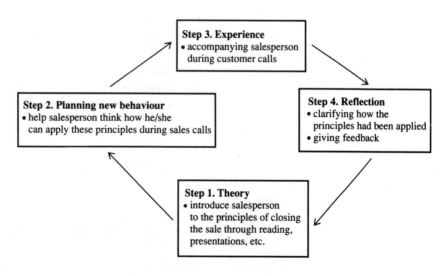

Figure 7.5 *Using the learning cycle to build sales closing skills: starting with the theory*

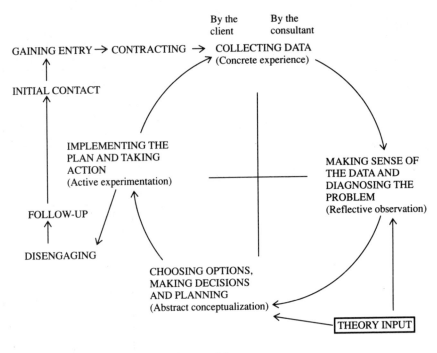

Figure 7.6   Learning styles and the consulting process

We believe there are five stages when using a theories and models approach. These are:

1 Collect data on the way the client or client system is dealing with the situation at the moment.
2 Identify a theory or model that will help the client understand the problem.
3 Make the client aware of the data.
4 Introduce the theory or model to explain the data.
5 Help the client make decisions.

Stages 3 and 4 are reversible. Sometimes you will need to introduce the data first and then explain it in terms of the model. At other times you will need to introduce the theory first so that the client is better able to understand the data in terms of the theory. An example of each approach might be helpful.

Example 1
Starting with the data

When doing team-building assignments we often use the group working model described in Chapter 6. This model, which categorizes team activities into task, systems and procedures, and process, is very useful in helping a team to identify where it places most energy and where any blockages exist. Rather than simply introduce the model 'cold' we generally ask members of the team to write down individually the answers to two questions:

• What behaviours, events, activities, etc. give you satisfaction and make you feel good about working in this team?

- What behaviours, events, activities, etc. frustrate you, make you dissatisfied or angry in this group?

This is the data-collection phase.

The next phase is to ask each member of the team to share his or her own list (data sharing) and these are written on a flip chart. Usually there is a huge list of events and activities. This in itself often leads to a great deal of useful discussion and insight.

Finally, the model is introduced in a way that helps the team to classify its own data in terms of the three categories. This helps them understand how their team operates. Very often they begin to recognize that many of the difficulties stem from process issues which are rarely addressed.

Example 2
Starting with the
theory

It is important to recognize that starting with a theory is not the same as teaching a theory for its own sake. The whole point of starting with a theory is to give clients a framework within which they can begin to understand the data. For example, an important element of our consulting skills seminar is to help participants develop skills in using all four consulting styles discussed in detail in Chapter 2. The starting point is to help participants familiarize themselves with the theory behind each style. This gives them a framework with which to examine critically their own natural style of interaction. They are then in a position to extend and develop their own approach when trying out each style.

Helping clients to plan

Having helped clients to make a decision, it is very tempting to rest on one's laurels. But making the decision is often the easy part. Clients will probably need help to think through the best way to implement the decision, and to do this they need to develop a plan.

A good plan should describe, in detail, everything that needs to be done to put the decision into action. It should include timing, people and other resources which must be marshalled and coordinated. It should include clear performance standards, production, service and quality targets. It will also include ways of monitoring progress and taking necessary corrective action.

There are many sophisticated planning and scheduling techniques available, often based on complex computer programs. This is not the place to describe these techniques. However, one very simple technique which can be used for planning is critical path method.

Critical path is based on the recognition that any project, no matter how complex, consists of completing a number of individual activities in such a way that they all fit together neatly. Thus, when preparing to run a training programme, the trainer may need to:

- do a training needs analysis by interviewing managers and potential trainees
- design the structure of the training programme

- choose appropriate training materials
- type and duplicate handouts, exercises, etc.
- identify managers who will run specialist sessions
- brief managers running specialist sessions on what will be expected of them
- arrange accommodation
- send out joining instructions to participants

Unfortunately, many of these individual activities cannot be started until other activities have been completed. For example, nothing can be done until the training needs analysis is complete. Some activities will take longer to complete than others and there will also be some sequences in which several activities follow each other. In fact, there is almost certain to be one sequence that takes so long that it predetermines the length of the whole project. For the trainer with the job of preparing the programme, this sequence might be as shown in Figure 7.7. This is known as the critical path: if the time to complete this sequence could be shortened, the whole project could be completed earlier, while if it took longer the project would be extended. All other activities can be scheduled around those included in the critical path as illustrated in Figure 7.8.

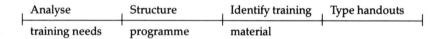

| Analyse | Structure | Identify training | Type handouts |
| training needs | programme | material | |

Figure 7.7   *The critical path*

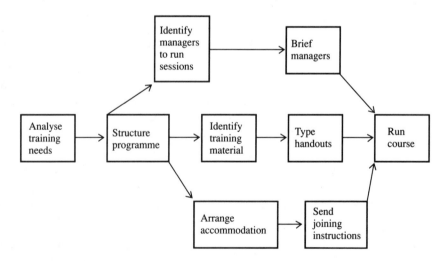

Figure 7.8   *A critical path analysis*

In our experience this technique can be of value as an adjunct to the planning process. However, we suspect you will also need an array of questions to help clients clarify the way forward. Such questions could include:

- What objective are you trying to achieve?
- When does it need to be completed?
- How will you know when you have been successful?
- What activities need to be carried out along the way?
- In what order do any activities need to be done?
- By when does each activity need to be completed?
- Who should do what?
- What are the budget limits?
- What other resources are available?
- How will you monitor progress?
- How will you communicate the plan to other people?
- How are they likely to react?
- What are the likely barriers to success?
- How do you feel about these barriers?
- How can the barriers be overcome?
- What can possibly go wrong with this plan?
- Who will this plan affect and how will it affect them?
- How will you ensure completion?
- How do you feel about this plan?

This list is by no means exhaustive. No doubt you can think of other items. Of course, the questions you ask will depend on the nature of the decision. What is important is that you move the clients on from decision making and galvanize them into action, so increasing commitment to the decision and the plan of action. To help you document and structure the planning process we have included a simple planning form (see Figure 7.9).

Goal						
Standards						
Deadlines						
Action steps	Who	When	Standard	Help needed	Resources needed	Monitoring

Figure 7.9 Action planning form

Summary

- Difficulties in organizations are not usually puzzles—they are problems and they rarely have a one-hundred-per-cent solution. Hence, helping clients could involve choosing between several forty-per-cent options.
- Real organizational problems are usually rooted in one (or more) of four interdependent focal issues:
  - power–authority
  - morale–cohesion
  - norms–standards
  - goals–objectives
- Helping clients to diagnose problems is often about clarifying, simplifying or restructuring the data. This can be facilitated by using data-presentation models such as decision trees and force field analysis.
- Theories can also be a powerful way of helping. However, if clients are to internalize a theory they need to complete the experiential learning cycle.
- When using theories and models, learning can start with either the theory or the experience. Both methods are equally valid and, provided the cycle is completed, will lead to internalization of the theory.
- Moving from problem diagnosis to action involves generating and evaluating options and planning. A good plan will describe in detail everything that has to be done to put the decision into action.

Feedback instruments

The following are examples of feedback instruments that you can use to provide feedback to the group or to help them give feedback to themselves.

1 The *communication pattern worksheet* is useful to record the frequency and direction of comments in a group. It can often illustrate quite graphically the differences between high and low contributors and the patterns of interactions.

2 The *group behaviour questionnaire* is useful to get group members to give feedback to themselves without your having to tell them what you observed. You can supply evidence to confirm or deny their assumptions about what actually happened.

3 *'What happened in the group?'* is a variation of the group behaviour questionnaire which focuses on different dimensions or aspects of group behaviour.

4 The *personal reactions questionnaire* can be used to help individual group members explore their relationships with others. Where the process issues are not being dealt with, this form can help you to bring them to the surface. Take care, it can be confrontational.

5 The *group systems and procedures questionnaire* might be useful if the group doesn't seem to have an appropriate set of systems and procedures.

Don't feel restricted by any of these instruments—process consultation and observation is a very individual affair. Do what you feel is right—and if all else fails, tell the group how you feel!

Instrument 1

Communication pattern—Observer worksheet
Frequency and direction of comments

Individuals being spoken to

	John	Mary	Jane	Simon	Bill	Peter	Joan	Alice	Group	*Total made*
John		✓✓✓✓✓								
Mary				✓✓						
Jane										
Simon										
Bill										
Peter										
Joan									✓✓✓✓✓	
Alice										
Total received										

Individuals making comments (row label at left of table)

The purpose of this observation sheet is to record the quantity of participation by each person and who speaks to whom. For example, in the simplified illustration above, after a few minutes of interaction we can see that John has spoken directly to Mary five times. Interestingly, Mary has not directed any comments back to John but has spoken to Simon twice. In the meantime Joan has made several comments but directed them to the group as a whole.

Instrument 2

Group behaviour questionnaire

This form is designed to help you think about behaviour in your group.

First read over the scales and on each place a cross against the number on the scale that typifies the behaviour of your group.

Write your reasons for your rating in the space provided after each scale.

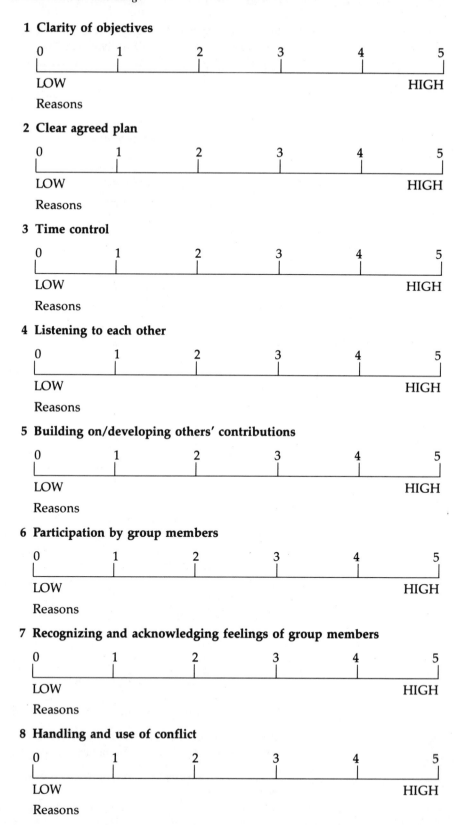

1 Clarity of objectives

| 0 | 1 | 2 | 3 | 4 | 5 |

LOW   HIGH

Reasons

2 Clear agreed plan

| 0 | 1 | 2 | 3 | 4 | 5 |

LOW   HIGH

Reasons

3 Time control

| 0 | 1 | 2 | 3 | 4 | 5 |

LOW   HIGH

Reasons

4 Listening to each other

| 0 | 1 | 2 | 3 | 4 | 5 |

LOW   HIGH

Reasons

5 Building on/developing others' contributions

| 0 | 1 | 2 | 3 | 4 | 5 |

LOW   HIGH

Reasons

6 Participation by group members

| 0 | 1 | 2 | 3 | 4 | 5 |

LOW   HIGH

Reasons

7 Recognizing and acknowledging feelings of group members

| 0 | 1 | 2 | 3 | 4 | 5 |

LOW   HIGH

Reasons

8 Handling and use of conflict

| 0 | 1 | 2 | 3 | 4 | 5 |

LOW   HIGH

Reasons

9 Quality of decision making

```
0         1         2         3         4         5
|_____|_____|_____|_____|_____|
LOW                                              HIGH
```

Reasons

Instrument 3

'What happened in the group?'

Consider the behaviour of the members of the group and answer the following questions by ticking a point on the scale for each question.

1 How far were the objectives clearly agreed?

NOT AT ALL 0...1...2...3...4...5... CLEAR AND AGREED

2 How far did members of the group generally agree with each other in order to reduce the tension?

RARELY 0...1...2...3...4...5... MOST OF THE TIME

3 How far did members of the group give each other information, opinions or suggestions?

RARELY 0...1...2...3...4...5... MOST OF THE TIME

4 How far did members of the group ask each other questions?

RARELY 0...1...2...3...4...5... MOST OF THE TIME

5 Conflict was apparent in the group:

RARELY 0...1...2...3...4...5... MOST OF THE TIME

6 How would you rate the level of trust and openness in the group?

VERY LOW 0...1...2...3...4...5... VERY HIGH

7 To what extent were decisions made by consensus?

NOT AT ALL 0...1...2...3...4...5... COMPLETELY

8 How far did the group use the knowledge, skills, expertise and resources of all the members?

NOT AT ALL 0...1...2...3...4...5... COMPLETELY

Instrument 4

Personal reactions questionnaire

Answer all questions with the *first name* of a group member. Base your nominations on your experience in the group. You don't have to answer all the questions.

1   Who influences me most in this group?   _____

2   Who is least able to influence me in this group?   _____

3   Who do I have most conflict with in this group?   _____

4   Who supports me most?   _____

5   Who seems to take up most group time?   _____

6   Who appears to lead this group?   _____

7   Whose contributions do I find most helpful?   _____

8   Whose contributions do I find least helpful?   _____

9   Who do I feel closest to in this group?   _____

10 Who avoids discussion with me?   _____

11 Who can I be most open with?   _____

12 Who am I least open with?   _____

13 Whose humour is helpful in the group?   _____

14 Whose humour gets in the way in this group?   _____

15 Who would I choose to work with?   _____

16 Who have I talked to least?   _____

Instrument 5

Group systems and procedures questionnaire

Make notes in the blank spaces provided. Record what happened.

Planning   How did the group start?

How did they agree objectives?

How did they identify the resources available?

What procedures did they develop?

Generating ideas   How did the group identify the information available?

What ideas were generated/rejected?

How were the ideas developed?

Control   How did the group stay on track?

How were decisions made?

What norms were evident?

Reviewing performance   How did the group review its own performance?

What ideas emerged to improve future performance?

8 Implementation

Why do clients fail to implement?

Implementation is the key phase in the consulting cycle. This is the time when the change starts to take place and people do things differently. The success of any consulting assignment hinges on the way it is implemented. Yet so often consultants' reports simply gather dust and are never acted upon, or implementation takes place in the teeth of severe opposition. So why do clients fail to implement?

To answer this question we must clarify what needs to be in place before implementation is likely to be successful. We feel that successful implementation depends on four factors:

Ownership the degree to which all the people responsible for implementing the change own it and are committed to it.

Leadership the degree to which senior managers are seen to be committed to the change.

Capability the degree to which people have the necessary skills to carry out implementation properly.

Organization the way the implementation phase is actually organized.

Ownership

The implementation phase of an assignment is likely to be uncomfortable for all those who are affected. This is because people are now required to make actual changes in the way they work. How they feel about the change is crucial and those feelings will be rooted, often, in the way decisions about the changes were made.

We often assume that 'change is uncomfortable' or that 'people resist change'. But is this always true? It is true that sometimes we feel threatened, uncomfortable, or even angry at the prospect of change. But there are other times when we feel excited by change, we welcome it and feel very positive about it. So what factors affect our feelings towards change? To explore this you might like to write a list of significant changes which have taken place in your own working (or non-working) life. Identify the ones you felt positive about and the ones you felt negative about. Then list the reasons for those positive or negative feelings. Use the chart opposite.

The factors that affect the way we feel about change can be placed in six categories:

Changes I felt positive about	Reasons

Changes I felt negative about	Reasons

- The amount of information we have about the change.
- The extent to which we participate in the change decision.
- The degree of trust we have in the initiator of the change.
- What kind of previous experience we have with similar changes.
- The impact the change is likely to have on our relationships with other people.
- Our individual personalities.

As an example, consider how you would feel if a senior manager brought in a systems auditor to check the efficiency of your department with the brief that his report will go direct to that senior manager without being seen by yourself. Our hunch is that you would feel pretty uncomfortable at this prospect. This is because the change has been managed in a way that scores very low on many of the factors we have listed. You have been given very little information about the reason for the audit, what the auditor is looking for or what will happen as a result of the report. You weren't allowed to participate in the decision to bring in the auditor. The initiator of the change was a senior manager and it is in the nature of organizations that the further apart people are in the hierarchy, the lower the trust between them.

Imagine, on the other hand, that your manager asks you to take on a project but offers to talk through with you the background and purpose of the project, how you intend to go about it and the help you need. This time you're likely to feel much less threatened because you have more information, you have participated in the decision and are likely to have more trust in your manager.

If you want to ensure a high level of ownership and commitment when your project is implemented then it is important that decisions which affect people are made appropriately. It may be necessary to discuss with the manager or management team the degree of involvement that their people will need in the decision-making process.

There are a number of styles available to the manager when undertaking a change programme. These styles are ranged along a continuum. At one end of the continuum the manager, together with the consultant, retains the responsibility for diagnosing the problem and making decisions which are then imposed on the rest of the group. At the other end of the continuum the people who will be affected by and required to implement the change are involved in both the diagnosis and decision making.

It is easy to assume that you, the consultant, would always encourage the manager to adopt a style of decision making which is high in involvement, because this will increase the level of ownership and commitment when it comes to implementation. But it is important to recognize that there is no right or wrong decision-making style. Sometimes it is appropriate to have a high level of group involvement in decision making and sometimes it is more appropriate for the manager to decide alone (see Figure 8.1). However, if we want people to feel positive

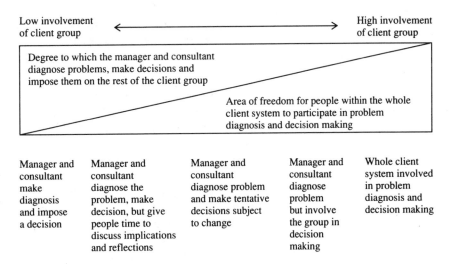

Low involvement
of client group

High involvement
of client group

Degree to which the manager and consultant
diagnose problems, make decisions and
impose them on the rest of the client group

Area of freedom for people within the whole
client system to participate in problem
diagnosis and decision making

| Manager and consultant make diagnosis and impose a decision | Manager and consultant diagnose the problem, make decision, but give people time to discuss implications and reflections | Manager and consultant diagnose problem and make tentative decisions subject to change | Manager and consultant diagnose problem but involve the group in decision making | Whole client system involved in problem diagnosis and decision making |

Figure 8.1 *Involvement of client group*

about a decision which affects them but in which they have not participated, it is necessary that:

• They have a high degree of trust in the person making the decision.
• They are informed as soon as possible about the decision and the
  rationale behind it.

So what are the factors that will determine an appropriate decision-making
style?

The **degree of emotional involvement of the group**. If the group members have a very high level of emotional investment in the decision, a
redundancy, promotion or a reorganization, for example, it may be
appropriate for the manager to retain a high degree of responsibility for
making the decision.

The **time available**. Sometimes there genuinely is no time to involve
everyone in the decision. If this is the case, however, it is important that
client group members are told the reasons for the decision and helped
to work through their feelings about it.

The **size of the client system**. If the client system is very large then it
may be impossible to involve everyone in every decision. In this case it
may be necessary to help managers and supervisors brief people in
small groups, tell them the reasons for the decision, allow them to think
through how they can implement their part of the change, the advantages and disadvantages for them, and how they feel about the decision.

The **degree of secrecy required**. There are some decisions which, for
commercial reasons, need to be kept secret, so only a limited number of
people can be involved. But these decisions are few and far between.
Some organizations, and some people, treat decisions as though they

are state secrets, when this really is not necessary. When it is necessary, the decision (and the need for secrecy) should be fully explained afterwards.

The **maturity of the group**.   There are some occasions when it is difficult to get a client group to participate in the decision-making process. It may be that they are accustomed to an autocratic style and are unable to cope with being more involved. It may be that this reluctance is simply a symptom of some underlying discontent—about the organization, the manager, the consultant or the proposed changes. Either way, this situation should be treated as exotic data which is likely to have a huge impact on the implementation of the project. You may find it necessary to confront this reluctance to become involved in decision making and explore it more deeply until the real issues become apparent and can be dealt with. You may often be involved in helping managers to identify an appropriate decision-making style which will maximize the degree of ownership that people have. You may well find it necessary to confront the manager and/or the group where the approach being adopted is inappropriate. This can obviously be a difficult and uncomfortable confrontation and needs to be handled very gently. Managers may find it painful to have to acknowledge that their behaviour is much more autocratic than they had believed.

Leadership

Leadership is another factor which is crucial to successful implementation. So often major organizational initiatives fail because key members of the management team simply do not believe in them. Organization development projects are doomed to failure, for example, if the chief executive makes it clear that he or she intends to remain aloof and unaffected by the whole process. What incentive is there for someone lower down the organization to be committed to change when the boss simply isn't interested?

As the consultant you need to talk through with managers how they are going to demonstrate commitment to a project. Whenever we embark on a total quality management (TQM) project, for example, we ask the senior management team to work on a number of questions:

- What do we want to achieve with TQM?
- What is a TQM employee? How does a TQM employee behave? How is this different from the way our employees behave at the moment?
- If employees are to behave in a TQM way what sort of management style is appropriate? How does this differ from the way our managers operate now?
- What are the implications of this for the board of directors, or senior management team? How do they need to operate differently if they are to support this change?

By answering these questions the senior management team begins to recognize that successful implementation of TQM depends on them as individuals and as a group being prepared to examine the way they manage the business and their relationships. Only when they accept the necessity to make changes in the way they operate can they reasonably expect the same from others.

Capability An assignment will fail if people lack the skills and competence needed to implement the change. Hence an important reason for failure is lack of capability. So what can you do if your clients are incapable of making the necessary change?

First, let us clarify what we mean by capability. Capability is the ability to do something well. This can be divided into three separate components (see Figure 8.2):

- a cognitive or *knowledge* level
- a doing or *behaviour* level
- an affective or *feelings* level

If I am to acquire a new skill I shall need a degree of knowledge. When learning to drive a car I need to know where the controls are, on which side of the road to drive, what various traffic signs mean and many other things. However, this knowledge alone will not make me a capable driver. I can never learn to drive unless I actually want to do so and feel confident about my ability. So to be competent in any new skill clients need the appropriate knowledge, an opportunity to practise the behaviour—to do it—and also the opportunity to work through their feelings about the need to change, about their level of knowledge and about their success or failure in practising the skill, i.e. in actually doing it.

This model is very useful when you are confronted with a client group that seems incapable of implementing agreed recommendations. It is helpful to find answers to the following questions:

- Do the clients simply lack the knowledge to carry out the implementation?
- Have the clients had sufficient practice with the new system?
- Is it people's attitudes and feelings which prevent them from being committed?

We have already seen that it is often the feelings component which is the most significant blockage to successful implementation. The clients

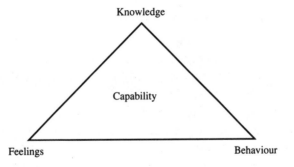

Figure 8.2 The capability triangle

might understand the new procedure, might even have the skills to carry it out, but if they feel resentful about being excluded from the decision-making process, or feel de-skilled by the new procedure, they are unlikely to give the change wholehearted support.

Organization   Projects will not be implemented successfully unless they are properly organized. Of course, the organization depends on ensuring that the implementation is properly planned.

The first thing to remember is that the people involved in the implementation of a project might come from different functions, different locations, different technical disciplines and perhaps even from different companies. If this is so they may bring past departmental conflicts to the project. They may be used to working to different procedures and rules. If the implementation team is very big there are likely to be communication difficulties. Imagine, for example, the organization required in a large construction project which may involve people in several different geographical locations coming from a large variety of technical disciplines.

It is important, then, when planning for project implementation, that attention is given to issues of teamwork, conflict and cooperation, communication, and the rules and procedures.

Low client commitment   We have already established that the commitment of the whole client system is crucial to successful implementation. You need to look for signs that will indicate whether your clients are really committed to change.

Before looking at our suggestions, write down your own ideas on how you would recognize low commitment among your clients.

Clients who are not committed to the change are likely to behave in any of the following ways:

Anger and hostility   Sometimes clients show signs of strong antipathy towards you and the project. Their hostility may stem from many sources: fears of inadequacy; frustration at lack of consultation; their anger may be rooted in some previous grievance and may simply come to the surface as a result of the project.

Objections   Often clients are able to identify many disadvantages to the project and are able to put forward objections without acknowledging any advantages. They may bring in previously undisclosed objections and appear to be moving the goalposts.

Unwillingness to look at the options   Sometimes clients are prepared to define and clarify the problem but are unwilling or unable to identify any possible courses of action. This may be due to a lack of ownership of the problem or a lack of commitment to doing anything about it.

Unwillingness to look at the process issues   Sometimes a client group is willing to acknowledge and work on systems and procedural issues but unwilling to confront the process issues which get in the way of successful implementation of change.

Hidden agendas   Where there is an unwillingness on the part of the client group to acknowledge process issues these may well emerge as hidden agendas. People may be trying to score points, settle scores or withhold information, all of which indicate that at least part of the problem is to do with such process issues. Real success is unlikely unless there is commitment to dealing with them.

Delaying tactics   When the implementation plan has been agreed, clients may find many reasons for delaying tactics: the time is not quite right; the priorities have changed; we need to respond to an emergency situation; we need to wait until after a reorganization, etc. Sometimes the reasons are genuine but often they are signs of low client commitment.

Failure to implement   The ultimate sign of absence of commitment is where the agreed action plan is simply not implemented by the clients.

There are many other signs that clients are low in commitment and no doubt you have identified some of them for yourself. However, the important question now is what you can do when you recognize low client commitment.

Dealing with low client commitment   It is very tempting, when confronted with clients who are not committed to a project, simply to collude with them. Collusion happens when there is an unspoken agreement to avoid certain issues, or to take the clients' objections at face value without risking the discomfort of challenging them and exploring more deeply. You may find yourself, for example, joining in with humour which is aimed at the project, the consulting team or management rather than confronting and exploring what lies behind the humour. It is important that you do not collude when clients display low commitment. Instead you need to explore the reasons for the barriers that exist. This can be difficult for clients as the barriers may be deep-seated and clients may feel vulnerable in exposing them.

When exploring low commitment you will need to use a range of consulting styles as described in Chapter 2. One option is to use a confrontational style. This is particularly useful where clients have agreed to take some action but have simply failed to do so for some reason. In this case you may be able to confront in a classic way by using words like: 'On the one hand you said that this project was important to you and you said you would take the action we agreed, but on the other hand you don't seem to be committed to actually taking action.' By confronting inconsistencies between clients' stated intentions and actual behaviour you will help them to acknowledge any barriers to commitment and make it possible to explore them further.

Often the causes of low commitment are deeply rooted in the clients' feelings, so you will need to use an acceptant style to help clients really examine their feelings about any future change, and start to deal with those feelings. Often, by acceptantly exploring the issues, you find that for the first time there is acknowledgement of the real problem or a dimension of the problem which has not yet been disclosed.

When dealing with objections to the proposals it may be useful to work catalytically with your clients. You can ask them to identify the advantages and disadvantages of the new system. This may help them to acknowledge that, while the system may not be perfect and could have disadvantages and potential pitfalls, these are outweighed by its potential advantages.

Consultant's role in implementation

Implementation is quite a difficult time for the consultant with many attendant ambiguities and dilemmas. The first dilemma is whether to stick around for implementation or disengage as soon as you have helped the client to make decisions about what to do next. This will depend on the original contract which may have been simply to help the client identify the problem, to gather data and make recommendations, and then to help the client plan the implementation of any recommendations. The advantages and disadvantages of staying out of implementation are outlined below:

Advantages	*Disadvantages*
• Ownership of implementation stays firmly with the client. • It maximizes opportunities for the client to learn and develop through taking responsibility for the agreed action. • It reduces dependency. • It frees the consultant for other projects.	• It is possible that nothing will be done. • The client may feel that there is no support. • Implementation may be carried out ineffectively or incompletely. • The client may not have as much expertise as the consultant.

Sometimes it is impossible for the consultant to remain involved throughout implementation. The trainer, for example, may contract to carry out an agreed off-job training programme but may find it impossible to follow everyone back to the workplace. If this is the case it is important that there is a strong contract with the line manager which ensures that the line manager accepts responsibility for debriefing, following up and offering support while the client works on implementing the learning back at work. So if you can't (or decide not to) be involved in implementation, before you disengage you need to ensure that:

• There is a solid plan for implementation.
• There is a high level of management support.
• There is a high level of client commitment.
• Everyone has the appropriate skills.
• Clients are clear about the circumstances in which they should contact you.

If you are to be involved in the implementation then the problem of the nature of your involvement still remains. Essentially, you now have two choices. You can take a hands-on role, carrying out the implementation yourself; or you can take a more facilitating and supporting role.

There may be times when it is appropriate to carry out the implementation yourself. There may simply not be anyone else with the time or the expertise. However, there are some important implications in doing this. The primary risk is that you are denying your clients an opportunity to learn how to solve problems for themselves. The other factor is the issue of control. By taking responsibility for implementation you are taking on the role of manager and taking control away from the real manager. By doing this you are actually reinforcing one of their suspicions about consultants—that they undermine the role of managers and take away authority and control. By reinforcing this suspicion you may well be creating barriers to gaining entry for other projects. So if you are taking a hands-on approach to implementation try at least to negotiate a contract in which you are responsible for no more than 50 per cent of the actual work and the client is responsible for the other 50 per cent.

The advantages and disadvantages of taking a hands-on approach to implementation are outlined below:

Advantages	Disadvantages
• It gets done properly.	• Denies the client a significant learning opportunity.
• It saves time.	• Engenders client dependence.
• The extra skills of the consultant are available.	• Low level of client ownership.
• Low risk for the client.	• Takes control and responsibility away from the manager.
• High level of satisfaction for the consultant.	• The change may not survive the departure of the consultant.

Perhaps the best role for the consultant during implementation is one of supporter and facilitator. When you are fulfilling this role, you are there to support and help but you never take over from the clients. In effect, implementation is treated as a second data-gathering activity during which you gather data about the changed behaviour within the client system and offer feedback to your clients. The facilitating role is that of observer, supporter, listener, coach and helper to the whole client system. You are there to check people's feelings about the new way of working, explore difficulties they are having, help them identify ways in which the plan might be modified and improved, surface any barriers that are still around, bring together parts of the client system that are still having difficulty working together and confront people who fail to implement their part of the new system. Acting as a facilitator rather than a doer at this stage is an empowering role that makes you available when needed, while freeing you to work in other parts of the organization. A checklist for carrying out this role is given at the end of this chapter.

The advantages and disadvantages of the facilitator's role are listed below:

Advantages	Disadvantages
• Empowers client. • Maximizes opportunities for learning. • Client can modify the plan with consultant's help. • Client feels supported. • Reduces dependency. • Consultant is able to oversee the project and bring the client's attention to any major difficulties. • Frees consultant for other projects.	• This is a more difficult role for the consultant. • The implementation may take longer.

You have, then, a choice of three approaches when entering the implementation phase of an assignment. You can:

• Disengage when the client has a clear plan of action and not get involved in implementation;
• Take a hands-on approach in which you take responsibility for implementation yourself;
• Take a facilitating and supporting role in which you act as an observer and coach to help the client come to terms with organizational or technological change.

All three approaches are used by consultants and can be adopted as appropriate. Generally speaking, however, the facilitating role is likely to be the one that empowers clients, increases their involvement and ensures that the change sticks.

Summary

• Successful implementation depends on:
  – Ownership
  – Leadership
  – Capability
  – Organization
• The degree to which we accept ownership of change depends on:
  – Information about the change
  – Participation in the change decision
  – Trust in the initiator
  – Previous experience of change
  – The impact of change on our relationships
  – Individual personality
• The appropriateness of decision-making style during implementation depends on:
  – Emotional involvement of the group

    – Time available
    – Size of the client system
    – Degree of secrecy required
    – Maturity of the group
- Successful implementation of change demands both commitment and leadership from the top.
- Successful implementation requires individual competence. Competence or capability is the ability to do something well and involves knowledge, behaviour, and feelings.
- Successful implementation also requires adequate organization.
- Clients who are not committed to the change may:
    – Show anger and hostility
    – Raise objections
    – Be unwilling to look at the options
    – Be unwilling to look at process issues
    – Use hidden agendas
    – Use delaying tactics
    – Fail to implement
- If clients demonstrate low commitment it is important to explore the reasons why.
- During implementation, the consultant may:
    – Stay out of the implementation altogether
    – Adopt a 'hands-on' approach
    – Adopt a facilitating role

However, of the three, the facilitating role is likely to be the one which empowers clients, increases their involvement and ensures that the change is permanent.

Checklist 8.1 *Implementation—taking the role of facilitator consultant*

If you want to take a facilitating and supporting role during implementation these are some of the things you might do:

- Provide support and encouragement.
- Observe and give feedback.
- Listen and offer counselling when things go wrong.
- Help clients plan modifications and fine tuning.
- Identify process issues which are getting in the way of successful implementation.
- Bring together parts of the client system to work on process issues, e.g. unresolved conflict, communication breakdown, etc.
- Help people from different disciplines, or from different parts of the organization, to work together.
- Prepare groups for change.
- Carry out training and education sessions with individuals or groups.
- Work with managers and help them as they support the change process.
- Open doors to other departments where their involvement might be helpful.
- Confront inconsistencies between the plan and what actually happens.

9 Disengagement and follow-up

What is disengaging?

Disengaging and (if necessary) arranging appropriate follow-up is the acid test of whether your activities have been effective. If the primary purpose of your consultation has been about initiating change then it is imperative that change is achieved and is not allowed to degenerate into a repetition of old patterns of behaviour. In this sense disengaging is the pinnacle of consultation. It is though, inevitably, a bitter-sweet experience. On the one hand it is the culmination of previous work, but at the same time it is the moment to start saying goodbye. Occasionally, you may be involved in follow-up activities to ensure that the change is consolidated. In other cases you may be engaged in constructing effective support systems but, in either case, disengaging is about completion and ending. Nevertheless, you are likely to find that the process has just as many pitfalls as any of the previous phases of the assignment and it is all too easy to stumble and fall at the final hurdle. For this reason the process of disengaging needs to be thought about just as carefully as initial contact.

Lippitt and Lippitt (1978) argue that 'a professional responsibility and goal of most consultants is to become progressively unnecessary'. This is the intention of disengagement. Although in some cases follow-up may be required, you should always aim to become redundant. However, this should be carried out in such a way that the organization or group is not left with a gaping hole which you previously filled. Ideally, disengagement should be a gradual process rather than an abrupt end. The only way you can ensure this is by raising the issue early in the relationship and then designing your intervention with disengagement in mind. This could include a number of options:

1 Involving and developing members of the client department to take over a similar role to the one you filled.
2 Agreeing during contracting a sequentially reducing time frame or budget for using your help.
3 Planning at the outset some form of terminal collaborative effort such as a report, article or publication to celebrate the end.
4 Agreeing a minimal support or maintenance plan—perhaps an annual or quarterly 'review of progress' meeting.
5 Agreeing an 'end point' celebration of what you and your client have achieved.

The central idea in this whole process is that every consultation must include some plan for the termination of the consulting relationship.

Furthermore, the sooner this is acknowledged and planned, the easier it makes the actual process.

Timing

Judging when to start disengaging is an important part of consulting skill. To help us make this decision we need to review the overall model of consulting introduced in Chapter 1 (see Figure 9.1). In this model we can see that under ideal circumstances disengagement should follow implementation. However, in theory, it is possible to disengage at any point after initial contact. This leads to several disengagement scenarios:

- If, after initial contact with a client, you find you are unable to gain entry, it could make sense to disengage from the assignment without going any further.
- Similarly, disengagement may be necessary as a consequence of being unable to agree a satisfactory contract.
- Your contract with the client could be simply to gather relevant data and then disengage—the client being left to make sense of the data and decide what to do.
- In other cases, your contract could involve helping the client to make sense of the data and diagnose the problem, but then leaving the client to make any decisions about what to do and to plan further action.
- Yet another option could be to help the client consider options, make decisions and plan what to do, and then leave, allowing the client to turn the decisions into action.
- Finally, the most satisfactory option (from the consultant's point of view) is when you agree to disengage after implementation of any decisions about action. Only after implementation can you be sure that any agreed action has been effective. Disengaging prior to implementation runs the risk that any change will not be maintained after your departure. However, staying beyond implementation runs the

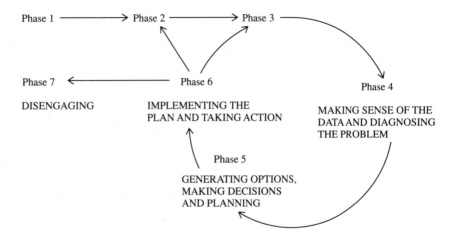

Figure 9.1   The seven phases of consultation

risk that you will overstay your welcome and as a consequence your relationship with the client will deteriorate.

When assessing the time to close an assignment (at whatever point in the consulting process) it is important to question whether you are avoiding anything by terminating at this point. For example, it is not unusual during decision making, or when you are trying to make sense of the data, for line managers to want to end a project if the focus moves from business or technical concerns to more personal issues (in other words, from the presenting to the real problem). There is a point in many projects where clients begin to recognize that their own style of management may be contributing to the problem. Furthermore, they may be reluctant to address the need for change in themselves. One way of avoiding personal change is to end the project prematurely. For example, during consulting assignments concerning total quality or customer care, data collection may lead to examining and modifying patterns of operation for the workforce. However, these are unlikely to be sustained without commensurate changes in management style and management philosophy. In both total quality and customer care assignments it is usually impossible to institute changes in how a workforce behaves without examining and changing the existing management style. It is not surprising therefore to find that some managers become fearful and seek to terminate the assignment prematurely without facing change themselves. Your task at this point is not to collude by disengaging but to find some way of supporting the managers and helping them face the discomfort, despite their wish to run away.

Similarly, if an assignment is going badly you may wish to terminate early and flee. Yet it is possible to turn a failure into an opportunity for development by asking your clients for feedback on how they see you contributing to the difficulty. Paradoxically, the more that you as the consultant are able to acknowledge openly any mistakes you may have made, the more your clients will feel able to trust you.

Having looked at some of the difficulties surrounding disengagement, it is important to return to the original question and examine how you know when to initiate the process. Essentially, this decision has two components: the first sets up an expectation of disengagement, the second marks the actual start of the process.

We believe that the expectation of an ending should be raised as early as possible with the client—and never any later than during contracting. The second decision, 'when to start', is more subtle. Fortunately, there are a few signals that legitimately indicate the need and these include:

- Recognizing that the contract has been fulfilled and needs reviewing.
- A reduction in the level of your direct intervention.
- Both you and your client recognizing that little more can be achieved and/or a mutual recognition that the client system needs to continue on its own.
- Your relationship with the client has developed to the point where you can leave the door open for further work as and when needed.

As soon as you are satisfied that these criteria are highly likely to be met you should start to move towards a close. If you expect to stay with the assignment until it is absolutely complete it is likely you will never leave (and as a consequence overstay your welcome).

How do I disengage?

Disengagement is initiated by raising and discussing with the client how you can withdraw from the assignment responsibly. As stated in the previous section we believe the time to raise this expectation is as early as possible in the consulting relationship. An illustration of how this can work in practice occurred for us some years ago. All three of us were involved in setting up a professional and personal development group for trainers within a large commercial organization. In order to get the project rolling we decided to use the services of David Casey, an external consultant, to help accelerate the group through some of the early difficulties in forming a new group. Before the start of the first meeting David wrote to each of the prospective group members. Among other things in his letter, he raised the issue of his own withdrawal from the group. He chose to do this in the following way:

Another issue I want to table now is withdrawal—my own withdrawal. I know I haven't started yet but that's when I like to talk about withdrawal: I would like the right to manage my own withdrawal, working jointly with the group, to get me out of your system as soon as we can, consistent with discharging my responsibility to help us all learn as much as we can. I know from Peter Cockman that your present commitment is to some sort of extended period of about a year, but that doesn't mean you have to have me around right up to the end. In fact the word 'end' may not be the right concept either.

This seems to us an ideal way of opening the discussion about disengagement and has influenced our own behaviour as consultants ever since. In effect it raised the issue of ending before the project had really started. However, in retrospect, it also highlighted a number of other points:

- It emphasized that the relationship with the consultant was finite—in some cases it could be for a fixed number of days, in others it could be until the implementation of some change.
- It immediately started to counteract any possibility of client dependency.
- It gave the consultant the opportunity to state clearly and assertively how he wanted to withdraw.
- It facilitated open and honest negotiation of any differences in expectations.

If you raise the issue of ending early, the actual start of your disengagement is inevitably less abrupt. Also it then becomes possible for both you and the client to use the process as a further opportunity for learning. This learning could involve:

- Checking out with the client the actual termination plan.
- Requesting an opportunity for both you and the client to give one another feedback on how the project was managed.

- Agreeing any end-point celebration/publication, etc.
- Contracting with the client about what may be required in the future.

The final closure of an assignment is also very important—particularly for internal consultants who may work in the same building as their clients and hence feel no need to close assignments formally. It is worth recalling the illustration we used in Chapter 1 where an internal consultant had been working with a client group over a number of months. As the clients' office was down the corridor from the consultant's, she felt no need to close the assignment formally. On the Monday following, the manager of the client group protested—in essence claiming that the consultant had not said 'goodbye'. Endings are as important as the beginning; saying 'goodbye' and 'thank you' is always vital (even when the client works next door).

Feedback

With all assignments, whatever point you select to disengage, it is important for you to obtain feedback, both as the assignment is unfolding and at the end. This is just as important with assignments that went well as with those that were not as successful; there is as much to learn from success as from failure. Given the importance of feedback it is essential it is planned as early as possible. Ideally, it should be included as a contract provision. This sets up the expectation with the client that you will be seeking feedback along the way and towards the end of the assignment. It then comes as no great surprise when you request it.

The feedback sessions are an opportunity for you and your client to learn from one another. Each of you needs to give the other feedback on your perceived strengths and weaknesses. It is important though, particularly when discussing weaknesses, that this is done constructively. Disengagement is not a time for airing grudges. If you and the client have been giving each other constructive feedback throughout the assignment neither of you should get any surprises at the end.

Is disengagement the end?

This is a particularly important question for internal consultants whose very existence relies on their being needed by other departments in an organization. It follows therefore that one of the objectives for internal consultants is to demonstrate their value to client departments such that they are invited back to do other work. Needless to say, all consultants experience some anxiety around disengagement (particularly if no further work is planned). Yet, paradoxically, we believe that the best way to ensure further work is, from the outset, to aim to become redundant. This means working to reduce client dependency to the point where you are no longer needed. Hence, our rationale for invitations for further work is based on a mature relationship that does not foster client dependency. On past experience as both internal and external consultants, we have come to recognize that this kind of approach is the best way of ensuring that clients feel comfortable about making requests for further work. This, we believe, is the essence of client-centred consulting.

Follow-up

Regardless of whether you are directly involved, some form of support or follow-up structure may be required to ensure that changes brought about during the consultation are maintained. Obviously, the precise nature of any structure will vary from one assignment to the next, but it is important that you have an overview of the types of structures which are feasible. These include:

- Planning for ongoing review of progress—if possible involving a wide range of staff from within the client system.
- Formation of support pairs or small groups which meet or keep in touch with one another on a regular basis.
- Documenting or reporting successful innovations through publications or professional meetings.
- Planning ongoing training designed to support change and/or introduce new staff.

It is worth noting that the internal consultant is in a very powerful position to provide follow-up support. By being present within the organization on an ongoing basis, you may be able to observe where further help is needed. However, while being more easily available, you do need to guard against engendering client dependency. Disengaging from an assignment with solid back-up and support structures in place is probably the best form of advertising for future work.

Transfer of training

Many consulting assignments for trainers involve running one or more off-the-job training courses for groups of staff. During these courses participants may be expected to learn about new or different methods of working which are to be implemented when they return to work. This transfer of learning from off-the-job settings to the workplace is always a problem in training. In many cases the transfer simply does not happen. Organizations spend vast sums of money providing training for employees, yet the changes intended are rarely fulfilled. This is particularly true in the case of management and supervisory training.

Over the years numerous courses have included sessions on leadership, management style, motivation, delegation, etc. yet their impact is often minimal. To understand why this has been the case we need to look at how many trainers choose to work. Usually the need, theme and content of training courses are agreed with senior management. From a consultancy point of view the contract is made with only a small fraction of the total client system. The groups who are to be trained are rarely consulted beforehand about intended changes. However, once the course has been agreed, the training department steps in and senior management usually have no further involvement until their staff return from the training. In effect the training department takes over the problem from management. Although the actual training may be sound, the difficulty is that the environment to which the staff return has not changed. Furthermore, it is highly unlikely that it will support the changes which the training course was intended to initiate. Not surprisingly, within a short period of time staff return to their old ways of working.

Although the case described may be oversimplified, the theme of the argument is accurate in many training settings. To overcome the difficulty we would urge anyone involved with training to behave more as a consultant: instead of taking problems *from* management, involve management in a more collaborative effort to carry through change. This will include working through what needs to be done to support the change when trainees return to the workplace, if necessary confronting more senior management on how they also need to change.

Summary

- Disengagement and (if necessary) follow-up is about ending an assignment responsibly.
- The main goal of a consultant is to become redundant—paradoxically this is probably the most effective way of ensuring further work.
- Ideally, disengagement should be a gradual process.
- All consultations need a disengagement plan—this means raising the issue of disengagement early (and no later than contracting).
- In theory disengagement can take place at any point in the consulting process after initial contact. However, to ensure that decisions about action are carried out, it is better to disengage after implementation.
- Beware of managers wanting to end a project prematurely if the focus shifts to involve them in any change.
- If an assignment is going badly, ask for feedback—this will probably lead to greater trust from the client.
- The disengagement can be split into two stages:
  - raising the expectation
  - carrying out the process
- Formally acknowledging the end of an assignment is very important for both clients and consultants.
- Plan for feedback—both as the project progresses and at the end.
- Internal consultants are in a powerful position to provide ongoing support.
- For trainers—problems with transfer of training can be tackled more effectively by adopting a consultancy approach.

10 Evaluating the consulting assignment

What is evaluation? It is tempting at the end of a consulting assignment to rush straight on to the next one. However, it is important to stand back and assess how effective your intervention has been. No doubt the assignment has involved a cost to the organization which could be measured in money, time or technology. There needs to be some way of measuring the degree to which the organization has gained a return on its investment.

Evaluation is the process of measuring how effective your intervention has been. This may sound simple but in reality it can be a complex business. One pitfall is that evaluation is done from the perspective of the consultant's professional discipline. For example, a training consultant may measure success in terms of a training programme, how well it was delivered and how much participants felt they learned. An IT consultant may measure success in terms of the elegance of the new system. A recruitment consultant may only be interested in the number of candidates that were attracted and whether an appointment was made. The danger in this type of evaluation is that there is no account taken of the needs of the organization and the client system. Client-centred evaluation asks whether the client's needs have been satisfied and whether the problem has been reduced or eliminated. Was the problem that was identified the real problem or a symptom? Was the solution that was agreed the most effective solution? Has the solution been successfully implemented?

No matter how professional a training programme, how well qualified a new appointee or how 'state of the art' a new piece of technology, none of these will be effective if they are solutions to problems that were wrongly diagnosed.

Hence, evaluation is a process which ensures that:

- The diagnosis of the problem was valid.
- The methods used for tackling the problem were appropriate.
- The methods used have actually made an impact on the original problem.

In addition it is also important to review how effectively the consultant managed the relationship with the client, how each phase of the consulting process was managed and how skilful the consultant was in the intervention. By doing this kind of review it is possible to learn and develop your skills as a client-centred consultant.

Purpose The main purpose of any evaluation is to maximize learning. Effective organizations are those which provide frequent opportunities for their people to learn, develop and grow. A consulting project will be a time of change, stress and challenge for everyone in the client system as well as for the consultant. By reviewing how the change was managed by all concerned it is possible to:

- Identify ways in which changes in the client system might be handled better in the future.
- Examine process issues that are affecting the client system.
- Clarify related problems which haven't yet been dealt with.
- Help the consultant examine areas for improvement when handling future projects.

It should always be remembered that, in a learning organization, people learn from their successes as well as their failures. They take time out to identify best practice, by the consultant and within the client system, so that this can be repeated or passed on to others.

Evaluating consultant success

Often consultants, and their clients, start to think about evaluation at the end of the project. We have heard of organizations deciding to evaluate training programmes which have been running for some time. The difficulty with this is that there may be nothing to evaluate against. There may be no record of the original organizational problem that the training programme was meant to alleviate.

The time to consider evaluation is at the beginning of the assignment, not at the end. It is crucial at the contracting stage to identify and agree what the real problem is, what are its causes and its dimensions, and how things will be when the problem has been overcome. Only when these kinds of questions are answered at the beginning of an assignment can it be properly evaluated at the end.

When you are assessing your effectiveness as a consultant, you need to be able to answer two questions:

- To what extent have we (you and your clients) made an impact on the original problem? (the problem and technology dimension)
- How well have you managed your relationship with your clients? (the consulting dimension)

As far as the clients are concerned, they want the problem solved, and they want it to stay solved. This is the ultimate 'proof of the pudding'. It is vital that a project is evaluated against the original objectives. In fact, you may argue that this is sufficient. We feel however that it is also important to review how effectively you, the consultant, have managed each stage of the consulting cycle, and how successful you have been at managing your relationship with your clients.

The flowchart in Figure 10.1 outlines the various parts of the consulting process against which an evaluation can be carried out. In reality, the 'problem and technology dimension' and the 'consulting dimension' are inseparable; they can't exist independently. However, if we are to evaluate every part of the system it is useful to review them separately.

Gaining entry It is tempting to see gaining entry as a discreet first stage in the consulting cycle. However, an effective consultant continues to gain entry with members of the client system. So if you are reviewing your effectiveness in gaining entry you should ask yourself not only about the barriers to gaining entry at the outset of the assignment, but also how your clients felt about you and the project throughout its life. The willingness of clients to accept feedback about the problem, their willingness to deal with process issues, the energy put into decision making and the commitment to implementation are a function of the degree of entry you have made with everyone in the client system throughout the project.

The contract—problem diagnosis There are two elements of contracting. The first is the way the problem is identified, diagnosed and agreed— the terms of reference of the project. The second element is the working relationship agreed between clients and consultant. Although in reality they are linked, we propose to deal with them separately as the first leads into the problem and technology dimension and the other into the consulting dimension.

The 'problem diagnosis' element of the contract should contain a clear definition of the problem in organizational terms. It should be a statement about the organizational pain or the improvement that is required. It should be stated in terms such as 'how to reduce the scrap rate' (not 'how to introduce better quality control') or 'how to project a better image and improve service to our customers' (not 'how to introduce total quality management').

A good problem diagnosis will include a statement of the objectives of the assignment, a picture of how things will look when the problem is 'solved', and some means of measuring success.

The contract—relationship with clients This element of the contract prescribes the responsibilities of clients and consultant. This contracting was successful if all parties were clear about their responsibilities, were committed to them and subsequently behaved in a way that was consistent with what was agreed.

Strategy and technology Having identifed the problem the consultant and client will determine the overall strategy or technology needed. If the problem is one of failure to meet a customer's quality requirements then an appropriate strategy might be to introduce new technology, a new quality control system or a total quality programme. If someone leaves a section the appropriate strategy might be to fill the vacancy with someone similar. Alternative strategies might be to restructure the department, introduce new technology, or buy in expertise. The question

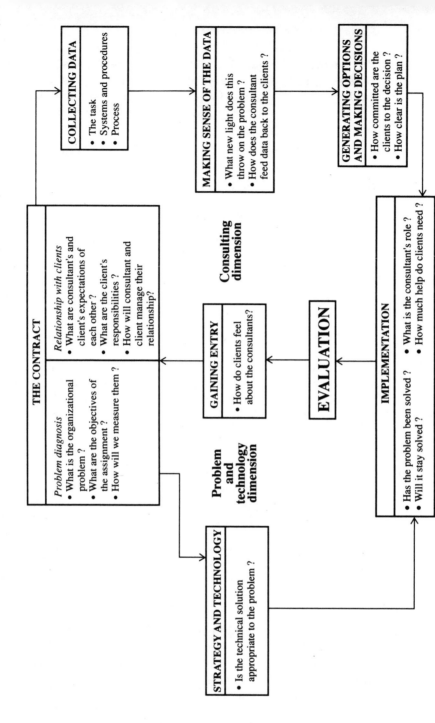

COLLECTING DATA
- The task
- Systems and procedures
- Process

MAKING SENSE OF THE DATA
- What new light does this throw on the problem ?
- How does the consultant feed data back to the clients ?

GENERATING OPTIONS AND MAKING DECISIONS
- How committed are the clients to the decision ?
- How clear is the plan ?

THE CONTRACT

Problem diagnosis
- What is the organizational problem ?
- What are the objectives of the assignment ?
- How will we measure them ?

Relationship with clients
- What are consultant's and client's expectations of each other ?
- What are the client's responsibilities ?
- How will consultant and client manage their relationship?

Consulting dimension

GAINING ENTRY
- How do clients feel about the consultants?

EVALUATION

IMPLEMENTATION
- What is the consultant's role ?
- How much help do clients need ?
- Has the problem been solved ?
- Will it stay solved ?

Problem and technology dimension

STRATEGY AND TECHNOLOGY
- Is the technical solution appropriate to the problem ?

Figure 10.1 Evaluation flowchart

to be asked at evaluation is whether the overall strategy was appropriate to the problem.

Collecting data   When evaluating the data collection you need to check the degree to which you stayed within the boundaries of the task and systems and procedures; to what extent you were prepared to surface process data about the way relationships were handled within the client system; and how you fed this back and helped your clients to deal with process issues.

Making sense of the data, problem diagnosis and decision making   You should help the clients to use appropriate methods of decision making and ensure that the clients take responsibility for making the decision. It is also important that you check the degree to which people affected participated in decision making and their genuine commitment.

Implementation—problem focus   At the end of the assignment you need to re-examine the situation. Has the original problem been solved or has there been a measurable improvement? Has quality actually improved? Have costs been reduced? It is also necessary to ensure that the improvement is permanent.

Implementation—relationship focus   If you are an effective client-centred consultant you will have worked hard during the implementation phase not to usurp the rightful role of the line manager. Instead you will have taken a facilitating role offering support, coaching people and giving feedback where the agreed action plans are not being met.

Evaluation   To evaluate your success as a consultant you must look in two directions. It is not sufficient simply to ask if the organizational objectives have been achieved; if you do this you will miss an opportunity to examine the intricacies of the consulting dimension of the project and thus to maximize the learning for you and your client system. At the same time if you simply look at the consulting dimension you could find yourself losing sight of what you were trying to achieve in the first place.

Who should evaluate the project?

As a client-centred internal consultant there are a number of people who have a stake in the work that you do. When evaluating a project it is important to gather data from all of them. Perhaps the easiest place to start is with yourself. You have been intimately involved in your work and your own reflections, recollections and feelings will tell you a lot about the success of the project. The questions in Checklist 10.1 at the end of this chapter will help you to evaluate every element of the project from your own perspective.

Another person with a stake in your work is your boss. As an internal consultant it is likely that the projects you are engaged in will be part of a larger departmental strategy. Your boss is likely to have a view on the way your work fits into the whole.

Your work is also likely to impact on your fellow consultants: people in your own department as well as consultants working in separate disciplines. If you have handled your project well, and created good relationships in the client departments, you will have enhanced the image of your own team and made it easier for others to follow in your wake. As part of the project you may have identified opportunities for other disciplines to help in the client department. Indeed, the most successful change agents recognize that the most effective organizational change tends to be multidisciplinary. For example, the same project may have planning, technological, human resources and training implications. Effective consultants are able to involve other specialists and work collaboratively with them.

We have left until last the people who will provide the most important source of evaluation data. This is because we felt that the last word in this book on client-centred consulting should go to the clients. Ultimately, it is on the way you manage your relationships with your clients that your success as a consultant will depend. It is important to remember that everyone who is affected at any stage of the consulting cycle is part of your client system.

So when evaluating a consulting assignment be sure to gather data about every element of the consulting process from as diverse a selection of clients as you can. Checklist 10.2 at the end of this chapter consists of a questionnaire which you may be able to use to structure information from your clients.

It seems appropriate to end this book by recounting a conversation we were party to several years ago. It concerned a young operational research officer who was about to leave the department to work in personnel. She was discussing the move with her boss who was saying what a valuable member of the department she had been and how much she would be missed. The young OR officer listened and said it was nice to be appreciated but, to be honest, the department was full of people who were much more qualified, more technically competent and more experienced than she was. Maybe, she suggested, the department would get along without her. 'Yes', replied the manager, 'it's true that I have lots of technically competent and well qualified people, but what I haven't got is many people like you whom clients ask back into their departments a second time.'

We hope that in some way the ideas in this book will help you to be the kind of consultant whom clients welcome into their departments not just a second time, but over and over again.

Checklist 10.1 *Evaluating a client-centred consulting assignment*

Gaining entry

- What were the boundaries of my client system?
- What were the major barriers to gaining entry?
- What strategies were used to gain entry?

- Which member of the client system was I most successful with in gaining entry? Why?
- Which member of the client system was I least successful with in gaining entry? Why?
- How much commitment was there to implementing the project?
- How do members of the client system feel about the new system now—at the end of the project?
- How do members of the client system feel about me now that the project is over?
- Who are the people in the client system with whom I feel most comfortable now?
- Who are the people in the client system with whom I feel least comfortable now?

The contract—problem diagnosis

- Did we identify the underlying organizational problem?
- Did our definition of the problem change as more data was collected?
- What were the stated organizational objectives of the assignment?
- What measures were used to indicate success?

The contract—relationship with clients

- How clear were my clients at the outset of the project about who was responsible for which elements of the project?
- How clear were my clients about how we would work together?
- Which elements of the contract did I fail to deliver?
- Which elements of the contract did my clients fail to deliver?
- Which elements of the contract needed to be renegotiated?
- Was there any element of my relationship with my clients that I was uncertain or uncomfortable about but which was not surfaced and discussed?

Strategy and technology

- What technological or oganizational strategies were used to overcome the problem?
- To what extent were the technological or organizational change strategies appropriate to the diagnosed problem?

Collecting data

- How involved were my clients in data collection?
- How much of the significant data collected was to do with:
  - the task?
  - the systems and procedures?
  - the process?
- How was the data fed back to my clients?
- Did the clients accept the data that was presented?

Making sense of the data, making decisions and planning

- What models were useful in helping the clients understand the dimensions of the problem?

- How committed were senior managers to the decisions made?
- To what extent were more junior members of the client system involved in decision making?
- How were decisions communicated throughout the client system?
- How committed to the decision were people throughout the client system?
- How detailed was the planning for implementing the decisions?

Implementation—problem focus

- To what extent have the objectives of the project been met?
- To what extent were the measures I chose appropriate?
- Has the organizational problem been solved?
- Will it stay solved?

Implementation—relationship focus

- What role did I take during implementation?
- How much help did clients need?
- How much responsibility for success did clients take?
- Will the new system outlast my disengagement?

Checklist 10.2 *Getting feedback from your clients—a questionnaire*

Consultant's name:
Your name:

What is your position and role within the department in which the consultant was working?

What was your involvement in the project the consultant was engaged in?

When did you first meet the consultant? What were your first impressions?

Was the consultant the type of person you had been led to expect? How was he or she the same or different?

Was the consultant the type of person you could trust? Why?

Did you feel that the consultant listened sympathetically to your point of view? Why?

How clear were you about what the project would entail, what your involvement would be and how you would be affected?

How much influence did you have on the decisions which affected you?

Did you think that the consultant was expressing his or her true feelings when consulting with you and your colleagues? Please give reasons.

Do you think you could rely on the consultant to act in a consistent manner?

How clear were you about your own role when the new technology or system was actually introduced?

How committed will you be to the outcome of the project when the consultant leaves?

Epilogue: Developing internal consultants

This section of the book is addressed particularly to those readers who have, as part of their remit, the training and development of internal advisers, from whatever department they come.

However well you, or someone else, do your actual training, the likelihood of it carrying over into the workplace is remote unless you get the diagnosis right and arrange for follow-up support. These aspects of training have been well researched and documented by Dr J.A.G. Jones (1985) of the Industrial Training Service Ltd. He calls these aspects of the training cycle:

Getting it right—making a good diagnosis
Doing it well—delivering effective training
Making it stick—ensuring carry-over into work

In our experience this analysis makes good sense for all training and trainees alike. It is even more important when trying to develop consulting skills for the following reasons:

- The change from trainees' normal way of working to being client-centred is often dramatic and challenging.
- Such change really needs to be embedded in and integrated with organizational change. Unless there is an obvious organizational need then the individual trainee is unlikely to be helped to sustain the change.
- Consultants have to be helped to learn for themselves rather than be taught. It follows that such experiential learning has to be continued after any off-job training so that the learning is continuous.
- Any change in personal style is likely to have an impact on the clients with whom the adviser interacts. This will probably mean that there is some pressure to stay the same. The adviser has to be confident enough to keep going in the face of such pressure.
- Unless the culture of the department or organization changes and adopts the new way of working for everyone, then the returning trainee is likely to find it difficult to sustain the new ways of operating.

Getting it right

It seems to us that making a good diagnosis is an aspect of training and development that is often ignored or treated rather casually; or the manager's diagnosis and suggested solution is agreed without challenge. Before anyone can be trained you need to know what deficiencies or difficulties are recognized in the department or the individuals, and how the training will help. So it is with consultants. It is therefore very important for the training and development people to be very clear and firm about their diagnosis.

When doing the diagnosis it is important to ensure that you identify the complete client system or as much of it as is within your reach. This could be one individual adviser in need of specific consulting skills. However, it is unlikely that this individual works alone and it will be difficult for him or her to implement the learning if it is alien to the existing departmental culture.

It is probably more effective, therefore, to look at how the whole department works with its clients at present and how this might change to be more client-centred. The whole department is now your client system and you will have to work with all the advisers and the manager to effect any lasting change. Even this may be too narrow a definition of the client system and you may have to look at other advisory departments within the organization. The reason we say this is that most consulting departments we encounter need help to work effectively together for the overall good of the organization. They are often very busy working from their own perspective without regard for all the other advisory departments who are doing the same.

Single issue initiatives
In our experience, most consulting assignments deal with what we call single issues. Generally, these are related to the main task of the client department, tend to ignore systems and procedures and process issues, and are often dealt with by a technical specialist without regard for what other change initiatives are going on within the department.

While such technical issues are usually very important for solving the immediate, presenting problem they have serious drawbacks in terms of effectiveness. The model of organization which appeals to us is illustrated in Chapter 6. This systems model remains in balance as long as it is not interfered with.

However, if even one of the facets is disturbed, by being worked on by a consultant for instance, then the whole model is affected. So if the work study department changes people's tasks and ways of working, then there is likely to be a significant impact on all the other facets. If the personnel department puts in a system of payment by results to reward individual effort, then there is likely to be an impact on everything else in the system. However hard the development department works to encourage teamwork it will fail unless both these initiatives are considered together rather than separately. Most large organizations employ a variety of consultants or advisers with different specialisms. Invariably they work in different departments and rarely integrate their work.

This results in considerable resentment from line managers who have a variety of specialist advisers all competing for their time and physical resources. These specialists can come from anywhere within the organization and range from audit and inspection through health and safety to training and development and it is left to the manager to coordinate all the different ways in which they are trying to help.

It seems to us that an important role for the training and development function is to help senior managers address these issues, especially when discussing the training and development of internal consultants. Some of the questions which need to be asked within this context are:

- How can we ensure that the consulting departments don't leave it to the line manager to coordinate their work?
- How can we ensure that all internal advisers direct their attention to organizational and process issues in addition to their client's task?
- How can we ensure that internal advisers collaborate across departmental boundaries rather than seeing themselves in competition?
- How can we get internal advisers to take a global view of the organization rather than a narrow departmental view?

When you ask such questions, you will probably find yourself confronting all sorts of power/authority issues within the organization and you may need help. Nevertheless, we believe that such questions have to be asked and the issues have to be tackled if the whole-organization approach is to bring increased effectiveness and continuous improvement.

We are not necessarily advocating the return of the organization development (OD) department. But it does seem to us that unless the single issues initiative problems are addressed then there is likely to be little real, lasting change within the consulting departments and the organization.

Assessing the need

It is important to assess the need from both organizational and individual points of view and from all angles. So before you draw up a detailed contract you will need to collect information about:

- how the manager sees the need
- how the advisers see the need
- how their clients see the need

You may also find it useful to get all three parties together to increase the manager's awareness and understanding of the real problems. In our experience, very few consulting departments have the courage to ask their clients what they think of the way consultants work.

You may also think it is important to establish whether or not there are genuine motivations for change, along the lines of Checklist 4.5, and try to assess how much commitment there is from the manager and the advisers.

Contracting

Once you have established the need you can probably move into contracting with the client system. It is traditional in most training situations

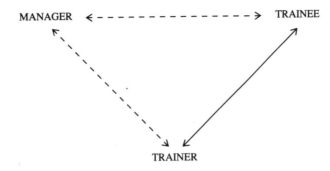

Figure E.1 *A training contract in which the manager has little responsibility*

for the line manager—the owner of the problem—to give up all responsibility for the training and its outcome to the trainer. So the contract looks like the illustration in Figure E.1.

The contracts between manager and trainee and between manager and trainer are either very weak *secondary* contracts or don't exist at all, while the contract between trainer and trainee is a very strong *primary* one. This has serious implications for all parties. The manager is able to abdicate and leave everything to the trainer. It also means that you are responsible for teaching and if the trainee doesn't perform better back at work you, the trainer, get the blame. The trainees can also blame you for not teaching them properly.

When working with a manager of a consulting department to help him or her develop the department, it is worth investing a lot of time and energy in negotiating a very strong primary contract with that manager. This should spell out the manager's responsibility for managing the change process. You may also need to help the manager agree a similar strong primary contract with the trainees. This will include the manager's expectations and the support to be offered to assist the changes, and should spell out the responsibility of the trainee for making them happen.

A better contract is shown in Figure E.2. Now the *primary* contracts are between manager and trainee and between manager and trainer and are very strong. That between trainer and trainee is *secondary* and temporary in nature.

This means that the manager retains ownership of the change which the training is helping to bring about. The primary contract between manager and trainer ensures that it is clearly understood and agreed that the trainer's job is to help the manager rather than to take over the problem. The secondary, temporary contract between trainer and trainee means that there is no permanency in the relationship and the trainer is not there to take over the manager's authority and responsibility. Neither is a dependency relationship thought to be in the long-term interests of the client. Above all, the manager retains ownership of the diagnosis,

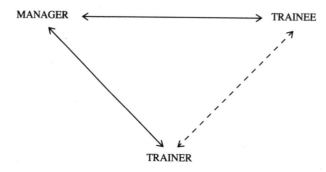

Figure E.2 *A training contract in which the manager is responsible for managing the change process*

can be encouraged to take an interest in how the training is done and is also committed to providing the necessary support to ensure that the training is carried over into work. Whether or not the manager actually provides the support is not your problem, although you may find it advantageous to offer your help.

Making it stick

Making it stick is the process of ensuring that the new learning is carried over into work. At first glance this would seem to fit logically after any formal training. However, in our view, attention should be given to it before the training begins. The essential steps are:

- Helping the manager make decisions about the most effective training format options.
- Helping the manager to contract with the trainees, to agree learning objectives and to indicate an expectation that the trainees will return with an action plan for continuous improvement.
- Helping the trainees to approach the training event in the best possible frame of mind and providing any pre-work assignment.
- Structuring the training event in a way that allows the maximum amount of time for practice, so that trainees internalize the learning before returning to work.

Choice of training option

We have assumed that consulting training is likely to involve some form of off-job event. In the chart that follows, we have highlighted some of the advantages and disadvantages we see for the various options.

It is also possible to train a team of consultants with their team leader either in-house or externally. This can often be useful in encouraging agreement over operating styles and enhancing team working.

We believe that when an organization has to embark on difficult cultural change it will generally need external help. Internal consultants who are locked into the existing culture are likely to find it hard to challenge without outside support.

Option	Advantages	Disadvantages
Single participants on an external event	Allows freedom on the programme	On their own back at work
	Uses cross-company similarities and differences	Takes a long time to get significant numbers working along the same lines
Pairs of participants from same department or organization on external events	Slightly restricts personal freedom on the programme	Possibility of support back at work
	Uses cross-company similarities and differences	Takes a long time to get significant numbers working along the same lines
In-house programmes for single departments	May restrict personal freedom on the pro-gramme especially if relationships are not all that good	High level of support for implementation back at work
	Can confront any insularity which may exist	Significant numbers can be trained at a time
		Doesn't benefit from cross-company contact
	Useful team-building bonus	May confirm insularity which exists
In-house programmes for whole organizations	Some restriction of personal freedom on the programme	High level of support for implementation back at work
	Can confront cross-department issues	Significant numbers can be trained at once
	Useful to enhance organization develop-ment	Doesn't benefit from cross-company contact
	Allows addressing of consultancy coordina-tion issues	May confirm cross-departmental boundaries and antagonisms

Follow-up Skill loss starts from the very moment the trainees leave the training environment. It is essential then that trainees go back to work with a high degree of commitment to changing the way they work with clients and begin to operate in the new way immediately. Before the end of the training event you will therefore need to encourage trainees to develop a detailed action plan which includes an assessment of the factors that will help or hinder the implementation and what can be done about them. It is similarly very important that there is adequate support back at work in terms of a manager who understands the need for changed behaviour, colleagues who will not laugh at attempts to change and clients who appreciate the new ways of working.

The next part of the follow-up must surely be to help the manager arrange for the necessary support. You may have to facilitate the negotiation between the manager and the trainees while ensuring that they all see it as their responsibility, not yours. If you go further than this and agree to arrange meetings or regular clinics you may find yourself doing what the manager should be doing. If you can help the manager to run the meetings or review sessions then that seems to us to be legitimate consultancy work for trainers. If you are an experienced consultant you could also offer supervision in the form of opportunities for advisers to talk over their experiences while trying to use their new skills.

Doing it well

We have left the delivery of effective training—doing it well—until last because, in our experience, that is the easy bit. As we have said already, you need to get the diagnosis right before you start to involve both the potential participants and their manager. Participants who are well briefed about why they are being trained and what is expected of them on their return, and who understand their responsibility for making it happen, are likely to be enthusiastic about the training before they start. Having said that, the training still has to be done well or the trainees' commitment is likely to be fairly low and their involvement minimal.

As far as possible, we adhere to the following principles when training consultants.

First, we prepare them as well as we can. We try to ensure that everyone understands exactly what is expected of them by giving them a comprehensive brochure describing the experience and a personal briefing at which they can clear up any dilemmas or concerns.

Second, we try to ensure that as much of the theory as possible is dealt with before the off-job event. This means that people are able to have as much practical, hands-on experience as they can get during the programme.

Third, we follow the principles established by David Kolb in his work on learning styles and experiential learning, as explained in Chapters 1 and 7. We believe that most people learn best what they experience for themselves but that they need to look back at the experience critically, reflect upon it, abstract useful insights from it and put the results to work.

Fourth, we try to ensure that people learn at three levels:

- a cognitive or knowledge level,
- a doing or behavioural level and
- an affective or feelings level.

Virtually every problem effecting a change in life is accompanied by some form of emotional response. Changing one's attitude and learning to do things differently usually involve considerable unlearning and are likely to invoke a similar response. Working through the 'feelings' content of any difficulty is an essential prerequisite to problem solving. So we try to ensure that participants:

- Acquire new knowledge and ideas about consulting skills, styles and processes.
- Practise the behaviour to put the ideas into action and experience how it feels to use these skills as a consultant and as a client.

Fifth, we always address all three aspects of our group working model: task, systems and procedures, and process (feelings). This means that, whenever a group runs into difficulties with its task, members are encouraged not just to put more effort or resources into it but to look for other reasons why they are having problems. In our experience the real problems or focal issues are more than likely to be in the process.

Sixth, we encourage the acceptance of the event as real. In other words, it is different from their normal environment and way of working but no less real for that. The issues raised between people are real ones, the fears are real and the ways of operating during the event are likely to be similar to the ways participants operate at work. Staying with what is happening 'here and now' provides very important learning opportunities.

Seventh, we try to get participants to accept that the off-job event is a consulting assignment rather than a standard training course. We then follow our own consulting cycle from initial contact to disengagement while using the skills and intervention styles with the group. To achieve this for all participants, the framework and timetable have to be flexible enough to ensure that everyone's needs are met as far as possible in exactly the same way as we would expect them to operate back at work.

As we highlighted in Chapter 1 we believe that consultants, especially those trying to operate in a client-centred way, need:

- Competence in the process of consulting
- A high level of self-awareness
- Competence in dealing with their own feelings and those of their clients
- A belief that clients have the ability to solve their own problems with a little help
- A thorough understanding of the ways in which clients are likely to behave as individuals and in groups
- A wide range of professional and interpersonal skills
- Sufficient flexibility of style to deal with a wide variety of clients and situations
- A real understanding of the helping process within the context of their professional discipline

We believe that the training and the follow-up should attempt to involve as many of these aspects of behaviour as possible.

Consultants often have to work in a large range of situations and therefore need to be able to adopt many different styles. During training we offer opportunities to practise these styles, understand the conditions under which each is likely to be appropriate and develop clear ideas about the risks involved for both client and consultant.

Where do we start? As in any consulting assignment we start by dealing with the problems and difficulties in making initial contact and gaining entry with the client group which has just assembled.

This is followed by contracting—finding out what everyone wants as individuals, what are the expectations of the seminar consultants by the group and vice versa. Contracts are also negotiated in subgroups whenever they work together.

How do we deal with consulting styles? Consulting styles are covered in the following way:

Stage 1 Participants share their pre-work to clarify their understanding of the style and agree ways of operating when using it to help a client.

Stage 2 Each person has an opportunity to practise the style with another participant as a client. They then receive feedback on the effectiveness of the intervention.

Participants are encouraged to present real, current and live issues. We do not use role plays as the element of realism introduced by real problems is extremely helpful to the learning of client and consultant.

Stage 3 After a period of individual reflection, participants discuss their learning from experiences as client, consultant and observer.

Stage 4 Participants come together with the seminar consultants to clear up any outstanding concerns or difficulties and look at opportunities for using the style at work.

Dealing with these concerns or difficulties in a larger group provides opportunities for everyone—not only the seminar consultants—to be consultants to each other, to work with another consultant and get feedback on their performance.

Collecting data Throughout the whole event participants are helped with their data collection from individuals and groups, using their observation skills and improving their listening. They are also helped to understand and use some of the data-collection and feedback instruments illustrated in Chapter 7. This data is constantly fed back to the participants and used to effect improvements during the event.

Planning for improvement Towards the end of the seminar participants receive feedback from their colleagues on their consulting skills as they have experienced them during the seminar, using 'Our Gift to You' explained in Chapter 7. From this and their own assessment they are able to develop an action plan to discuss with their manager to effect a continuous improvement back at work.

Implementation Towards the end of the seminar participants have two opportunities to carry out complete consultations during which they work through all the phases of the consulting cycle. In the first of these each participant has an opportunity to be a consultant to a small group, using a theory or model to help the group make sense of the way they have operated throughout the seminar and decide how they might be more effective.

In the second opportunity everyone is a consultant to a colleague, using either a significant work-related problem which is causing concern or working on the difficulties that might be encountered back at work while trying to implement what has been learned.

In all situations participants are free to make a contract with their client and then apply the strategy and intervention styles that seem most appropriate in helping the client to solve his or her problems.

Disengagement As has been said earlier in this book, disengagement is important for both client and consultant and if, during the assignment, you have built a strong relationship it can sometimes be very difficult. Saying 'goodbye' is often very hard. We try to make it as painless as possible and see it as a celebration, an opportunity to share commitment to action, thank people for their help and arrange possible follow-up.

It is also a good opportunity to remain within your own model and ask for feedback on your performance. If you have managed to establish a culture which has provided constant, ongoing feedback you shouldn't get any surprises. Nevertheless, sometimes we do!

Our final plea to you as a training and development consultant is this: If you are there to help other consultants become more client-centred you will have to work that way with them yourself. Whether you are doing the diagnosis, delivering the training, facilitating its transfer back to work or all three, stay firmly client-centred. They may not like it, they may try to pressurize you out of it, but it will work. You will leave the problem where it belongs—with the clients—while you work hard to help them solve it.

Bibliography

Blake, R.R. and J.S. Mouton, *Consultation: A Handbook for Individual and Organization Development*, Addison-Wesley, Wokingham, 1983.

Block, P., *Flawless Consulting: Guide for Getting Your Expertise Used*, Learning Concepts, Austin, Texas, 1983.

Crum, T.T., *Magic of Conflict: Turning a Life of Work into a Work of Art*, Simon & Schuster Inc., New York, 1989.

Honey, P. and A. Mumford, *Manual of Learning Styles*, Peter Honey, Maidenhead, 1986.

Jones, J.A.G., 'Training Intervention Strategies', *Training and Development*, February 1985.

Kolb, D.A., *Learning Style Inventory*, McBer & Co., Boston, 1985.

Lewin, K., *Field Theory in Social Science*, Harper & Row, New York, 1951.

Lippitt, G. and R. Lippitt, *The Consulting Process in Action*, University Associates, U.S., 1978.

Phillips, K. and P. Shaw, *A Consultancy Approach for Trainers*, Gower Publ. Co., Aldershot, 1989.

Revans, R.W., *Action Learning—New Techniques for Managers*, Blond and Briggs, London, 1980.

Sargent, P.B., *A Decision Tree Approach to Case Study Solution*, NEBSM, 1979.

Index